THE THEOI
AS PREACHER

THE THEOLOGIAN AS PREACHER

Further sermons from Colin E. Gunton

COLIN E. GUNTON

EDITED BY

SARAH J. GUNTON
AND
JOHN E. COLWELL

INTRODUCTION BY

STEPHEN R. HOLMES

t&t clark

Published by T&T Clark
A Continuum imprint
The Tower Building, 11 York Road, London SE1 7NX
80 Maiden Lane, Suite 704, New York, NY 10038

www.continuumbooks.com

All rights reserved. No part of this publication may be reproduced or transmitted in any form or by any means, electronic or mechanical, including photocopying, recording or any information storage or retrieval system, without permission in writing from the publishers.

Copyright © Sarah Gunton and John Colwell, 2007

British Library Cataloguing-in-Publication Data
A catalogue record for this book is available from the British Library

ISBN-10: 0–567–03121–7 (paperback)
ISBN-13: 978–0–567–03121–1 (paperback)

Typeset by Kenneth Burnley, Wirral, Cheshire
Printed on acid-free paper in Great Britain by MPG Books Ltd, Bodmin, Cornwall

Contents

Preface
    Sarah J. Gunton   vii

Foreword
    Members of Brentwood United Reformed Church   ix

Introduction
    The Theologian as Preacher, the Preacher as Theologian
    STEPHEN R. HOLMES   xi

The Sermons

1. *The Creed (1) Creation* (Genesis 1.1)   3
2. *The Creed (2) Belief and the Role of the Church* (Mark 9.24)   11
3. *The Creed (3) God's Covenant* (Hebrews 1.15)   17
4. *The Creed (4) Normality and the Image of God* (Luke 24.39–40)   23
5. *Prophets and Apostles* (Malachi 3.1)   31
6. *The Worldly Christ* (Hebrews 10.5)   37
7. *Materialism* (Romans 12.1)   43
8. *Heaven and the Saints* (Revelation 21.12, 14)   49
9. *Christianity and Islam* (Matthew 2.1b)   55
10. *The Problem of Evil* (Isaiah 45.6, 7)   61
11. *Prophecy and Proof* (Matthew 2.23)   67

12	*Eternal Punishment* (Romans 11.29)	75
13	*Secular and Divine Power* (Revelation 5.12)	81
14	*Jesus, the Second Adam* (Mark 1.12–13)	87
15	*Prophecy* (Revelation 1.19)	95
16	*Death and the Resurrection* (Revelation 20.13)	101
17	*Death and Modernity* (Romans 13.8)	109
18	*Death and Readiness* (Psalm 90.12)	115
19	*Life and the Spirit* (Revelation 22.1–2a)	121
20	*The Trinity and Worship* (John 15.26)	127
21	*The Meaning of Love* (Genesis 29.20)	133
22	*The Resurrection and the Ascension* (John 20.17)	139
23	*Ascension and the Perfect Sacrifice* (Hebrews 10.12)	145
24	*The Remission of Sin* (2 Corinthians 5.21)	151
25	*Judgement* (1 Corinthians 1.7)	159

Index of Biblical References   165

Preface

My father died very suddenly and unexpectedly in his sixty-third year. He had always planned to publish a second volume of sermons, and we have set out to honour his intention by producing this volume.

Reference is made to my father's 'untimely death'. I believe that it was not untimely and that he would have agreed with me (as is clear from a number of the sermons in this book) and with the sentiments expressed in the following statement attributed to Jack London:

> I would rather be ashes than dust!
> I would rather that my spark should burn out in a brilliant blaze than it should be stifled by dry rot.
> I would rather be a superb meteor, every atom of me in magnificent glow, than a sleepy and permanent plant.
> The proper function of man is to live, not exist.
> I shall not waste my days in trying to prolong them.
> I shall use my time . . .

My father was an enthusiast – for many things, life included – and, in his enthusiasm, tended to repeat himself. This is reflected in the recurrence of anecdotes in his sermons over time, and I have chosen to smile to myself at the repetitions rather than to edit them out. I hope that this gives you a flavour of the man, rather than proving an irritation.

Reviewing the piles of hard-copy sermons meticulously stored in my father's study has been a rewarding experience. At one level I had the pleasure of seeing his handwriting again and picturing him making working amendments in the course of giving the sermon itself. At another, I engaged with the sermons in a totally different way as a result of reading, selecting and ordering them and, in some cases, copy-typing them. I also know that he would have been delighted by the fact that I flipped through the Bible he gave me in childhood and his hymn book in order to complete or verify the citations.

I would like to thank John Colwell and Stephen Holmes, both former students and friends of my father, for their help in producing this book. As a lawyer whose main contact with works of theology has been the first chapter or so of each of her father's books, I was not perfectly qualified to complete the task. I would also like to thank my sister, Carolyn, who began the task of ordering the sermons and who therefore made my job more straightforward.

SARAH J. GUNTON

Foreword

Colin Gunton was Associate Minister at Brentwood United Reformed Church from 1975 until his untimely death in 2003. Here he found a sphere and a community in which his faith, his theology, his intellectual brilliance and his deep understanding could find new and fruitful expression. He preached monthly during most of that period – a period during which his academic career developed so remarkably, with many books, many research students and many demands to travel and teach. He was a theologian who was always searching for the truth about God, and he shared that journey with us. We, as the local community of God's people to which he belonged and which he loved so much, also contributed to his theological journey, although we were largely unaware of that.

Colin's sermons in the early days were often hard to understand, and some complained they were 'academic'. As the years passed, what Colin experienced in the local church and in society in general was clearly in dialogue with his theological journey. The issues facing the life of the local church – to stay in the town centre or move to a housing estate, the nature of our mission to those who hired our building, the death of the young, children at communion – were not just used as practical examples, but Colin, the theologian, had reflected deeply and biblically on them. It was the same with issues facing society at large: genetic engineering, integrity in public life, the relentless pressure on time. His sermons were often an uncompromising interpretation of the biblical passage for the day, and he latterly railed against modernity, but he fed us with the ultimate hope of the Gospel.

For those of us who listened to his finely crafted sermons,

the quality of his life among us added an important dimension. Colin was not a man who thought too highly of himself. Although forthright and often confrontational in argument with fellow academics, and sometimes with church friends, Colin was always as much a learner as a teacher. Having argued vehemently, he would, on many occasions, then grant the point and return to the discussion at a later date having thought further. He took the insights of 'ordinary' church members very seriously, but he cared too much about the pursuit of truth to be comfortable with different views on important matters. However, the command 'Love one another, as I have loved you' was paramount, and we knew him as a man who practised what he preached.

Colin had a zest for life that inspired hope even in dark times. He was an enthusiast for so many of the things that enrich life – music, theatre, his garden, cricket, church social gatherings, children in church, good books, fine hymns (especially Isaac Watts), family holidays – and his enthusiasm was infectious. But in times of doubt and anxiety he insisted on the bare hope of the Gospel. When small numbers at evening services made them seem unviable, he reminded us quite sharply that the little congregation was worshipping in the presence of angels and archangels.

During the 1980s, as we prepared for our first open day, Colin gave us a definition of the Church to put on a large banner in the entrance hall. It said, 'The Church is a community of all ages called to praise God in worship and in life'. Worship and life, theology and daily Christian living – Colin always sought to hold these together in his own life and to help us to do so in ours. As you read these sermons, remember that their author was a good man who practised what he preached.

TONY CHEER
SHEILA MAXEY
CHARLES STEYNOR
Members of Brentwood URC

Introduction
The Theologian as Preacher, the Preacher as Theologian

STEPHEN R. HOLMES

I

I think he was quoting someone else, but I remember more than once Colin Gunton saying to me, 'You can always tell when a theologian has stopped preaching; their work loses something vital'. In one of those conversations it became clear that two or three sermons a month, all newly written, was the bare minimum that any real theologian was to manage. Whether a borrowed observation or not, the idea is entirely characteristic of Colin. Theology, he believed passionately, was the church's science – pointless and meaningless if not directed to the maintenance, edification and extension of the body of Christ. That this worked itself out particularly through the pulpit was, of course, a function of Colin's distinctively Reformed theological vision: preaching was for him the central act of the church's ministry in important ways. In part too, it reflected the fact that Colin took with utter seriousness his congregational heritage. It mattered, decisively, to him not just that he was connected to some vague metaphysical ecclesial entity but also that he was in active membership of a local church where he knew his sisters and brothers in Christ and they knew him. And, of course, Colin had learnt his theology in part from reading Karl Barth, and the living, active, preached Word of God was something that he believed in with passion. So for Colin, coming to theology with this

Reformed and Congregational background, the maintenance, edification and extension of the church was accomplished primarily by the faithful preaching of the Word of God by, in and to local congregations.

This book is testimony, if any were needed, to the fact that Colin Gunton never stopped preaching. For decades he served as Associate Minister to Brentwood United Reformed Church, and once or twice a month at least he cheerfully accepted the call to preach to his people. Those of us who worked with him know how often a conversation in a seminar or over coffee would begin with Colin reflecting on the text of Scripture set by the lectionary, or on a conversation in last night's Bible study. I have been asked, by way of an introduction to this new collection of Colin's sermons, to explore the import of such comments and so to offer some brief reflections on the relationship between theology and preaching in Colin's life and work.

II

It happens that I never had the privilege of hearing Colin preach. Several times, however, I was able to accept his invitation to preach at Brentwood, and Heather and I would join him, Jenny and a large gathering of others from the fellowship for a fine lunch afterwards. Somehow, those days were always memorable: one time, conversation over lunch turned to the possible origins of a stream of water which intermittently ran through the garden, leading to five or six of the menfolk, all still in Sunday suits, spending the afternoon lifting every drain cover in the street to try to plot how the water board were dealing with the run-off from the wood behind the houses; another service coincided with Colin and Jenny's choral society singing *The Dream of Gerontius*, culminating in another throng of guests in their living room and Colin, flushed with the excitement of the performance still, declaring to all alternately the glories of Elgar's music and the horrors of Newman's theology.

Two recollections are more germane to the theme of this book, however. For a first, perhaps the moment there that

Introduction

made the most impression on me in all my visits to Brentwood, despite its being so fleeting, was a comment in passing from a member of the church as Colin swapped a gin and tonic for his coat on the doorstep. The man – I forget his name – said, with a note of pleased surprise in his voice, 'I was on the Internet last night Colin and I saw you'd written a book'.

At the more congregational end of church life, where there is a strong focus on the importance of the local church and on the relationships within that fellowship, we tend to talk a lot about 'the church family'. Like a family, within the fellowship there is perhaps a quiet pride in the professional and public achievements of members but also a certain discounting of them. What matters is who you are in the family, the relationships and roles you enjoy there. I suppose that this man was perhaps fairly new to the church and that most people in Brentwood were aware of Colin's intellectual eminence, but that did not define his role within the fellowship in any serious way (other than perhaps, giving more legs to annual jokes in the church Christmas entertainment about not understanding his sermons). The call to preach does not come from having greater knowledge than others; it comes from God, through the local church. Colin's preaching was service to the church he was a part of, at the request of that church.

This notion of what it is to be a church is repeatedly recalled and rehearsed in these sermons. As we read them, we are overhearing contributions to a family's conversation. Contributions of a particular and formal sort, to be sure, but they belong to the family nonetheless. There are passing references to events in the life of the church, or to something someone else has said or done (referenced as 'Charles' or 'Robert' of course; what else is necessary in the family?), which indicate how bound up this preaching was in the common life of the fellowship; the church is discussed in detail in different ways in at least two of the sermons: 'Belief and the Role of the Church' stresses the nature of Christian fellowship, and 'Prophets and Apostles' describes the particular ministry of elders within the

United Reformed Church. The moment this realization struck me most strongly, however, was reading the comments about the commercialization of Christmas in the sermon on 'The Worldly Christ'. After acknowledging all the usual complaints about what Christmas (or, more precisely, Advent) has become, Colin simply comments 'I continue to enjoy it, largely because of this community . . .'

A second recollection: I remember my first visit to Brentwood – still a Ph.D. student – and feeling a certain degree of trepidation about preaching in front of Colin. Brentwood followed the old Reformed practice of processing in a Bible at the beginning of the service; the first words spoken were to be from Scripture, as God through his word invited us to worship, and the service proceeded along the classical Reformed pattern of Scripture being heard and responded to, heard and responded to, with response as praise or prayer or offering or commitment as the need may be. Colin said to me in connection with that service, 'you should always have three readings from Scripture – Old Testament, New Testament and Gospel – and a psalm at the beginning. After all, it is only when the Bible is being read that you can be sure God is speaking to the people!' I never did quite work out if this was a gentle and generous criticism of the sermon I preached, or a more general comment, but it highlights the only meaningful genius of Reformed theology, and one to which Colin held firmly. In the Scriptures we find the *viva vox Dei*, the living voice of God.

The idea that the Bible contains the word of God is, of course, a common enough one in theology, and an endlessly disputed one. As these sermons illustrate, for Colin this was not any simple or abstract principle. The attitude to the text of Scripture displayed here is perhaps best characterized as one of respectful, patient, *attention*. Resisting both the 'conservative' temptation to grasp too rapidly at a possible meaning and stridently to insist on its truth, apparently oblivious to attendant difficulties, and the 'liberal' temptation to dismiss too rapidly a difficult or obscure text as meaningless, irrelevant, or out-dated, Colin transparently lived and struggled with the text of Scripture, seeking meaning and truth for his people. One interesting example of this is found in the sermon on 'Normality and the Image of God', the sermon Colin preached just two days before his death. Faced with the repeated claim in Luke 24, that the death and resurrection of Jesus happened 'according to the Scriptures', there is no attempt to find a half-convincing prediction buried somewhere in the minor prophets, nor is there a dismissal of the text as a witness to naïve, pre-modern reading practices. Rather, noting the particular claim of the text that it is the great sweep of the Old Testament that witnesses to Jesus' ministry and resurrection, Colin offered two interesting interpretative possibilities for making sense of the text, possibilities that make a difference to our understanding of the great purposes of God. A textual difficulty here is, therefore, not an arid 'Bible difficulty' which needs solving to shore up the weak faith of the congregation, nor is it something to be passed over as if it did not matter. Instead, it is an invitation to deeper thought as to what is really going on and so leads to a solution that serves to build up the church.

Another instance is found, almost in passing, in the sermon on 'The Worldly Christ'. The third reading has been from Colin's favourite book of Hebrews and contained the line 'Sacrifice and offering you did not desire, but a body you prepared for me' – a quotation from Psalm 40.6–7, which follows the majority reading of the Greek translation of the Old Testament, rather than the Hebrew (and some manuscripts of the Greek), and then adjusts the sense even of that to a certain extent. Colin simply resisted the temptation to be embarrassed by this, commenting straightforwardly, 'In point of fact, our author is rather mistranslating a Psalm there, but it does not matter, for it is what he does with it that counts'. In a stricter literary form than sermon this might have been phrased as a comparative, rather than a disjunction ('the mistranslation matters less than the meaning found by the author'), but the point is still joyously right: what matters for the preacher, of all people, is the truth taught by Scripture, not boring puzzles about its prehistory.

As a last example, consider the fascinating treatment of the 'three wise men' in the sermon entitled 'Christianity and Islam'. Here, there is really no problem to be solved, but instead a tradition of interpretation which is in danger of obscuring the meaning of the text. With patience and generosity, Colin unpicks both what the text really has to say to his congregation and the noble reasons behind the unhelpful accretions which he is clearing away. Here Colin not only displays once again respectful attention to the text, he is also gracious towards those who developed the interpretation he is unpicking, noting the true and worthwhile messages that were carried by it in a delightful way, through his reading of Jan Gossaert's great painting.

If patient attention is necessary to find meaning in text, respectful attention is demanded by the authority of the text. The attitude to Scripture displayed in these sermons is not just a belief that it might, occasionally in spite of all appearances, have something to say; there is also a conviction that, just because it is Scripture, what it has to say demands to be listened to. There are flashes of the sort of close attention to the detail of the text that is sometimes embarrassing to modern scholarship, seen as overinterpretation. But, of course, it is only overinterpretation if we assume the text is not pregnant with meaning from the start. So Colin lights upon the apparently incidental detail that, in John's account, Mary mistakes the risen Lord for the 'gardener' to make a telling point about the relation of Jesus to the first gardener, Adam. Furthermore, and, strikingly perhaps, it is not just the teaching of Scripture, but its shape, not just the answers it gives to questions, but the way it chooses to ask them, that must be taken with utter seriousness. 'I would not have raised the question in this way were it not a properly biblical

Introduction

question to raise', Colin announces at one point ('Eternal Punishment').

A final comment on Colin's attitude to the Scripture in these sermons: the interactions between the three Scripture passages read for each are instructive. In classical Reformed hermeneutics there is a principle known as the 'analogy of faith' (*analogia fidei*) which, at its simplest, is a claim that more difficult passages of Scripture should be interpreted in conformity with clearer ones. (It is also a claim about the place of theology in interpreting the Bible, but more of that later.) Such a simple claim presumes much, notably that the message of Scripture is unitary, if not uniform, and so texts from widely differing authors, dates and literary genres can be brought into meaningful conversation. This can be seen happening in many of these sermons in instructive ways. At the beginning of his sermon on 'The Spirit', for instance, there is a revealing hint of how passages were chosen for these sermons: 'I looked again in preparation for this sermon at the central verses of the account of creation in Genesis 1, and might have used it for the Old Testament reading had not the Ezekiel passage, to which we shall come, seemed more appropriate to go with the verses from John which we heard'. Texts that belong together, interpret and support each other, are much in evidence here. The 'appropriateness' between the two texts here turns first on the fact that they use similar metaphors to speak of the Spirit, but careful reading of the sermon, and the texts, suggests it goes deeper than that. As the sermon develops, an account of the work of the Spirit in creation is drawn from the common image; the passage from the Gospel of John is used to speak of the Spirit's work in redemption; and then Ezekiel is invoked for the Spirit's eschatological work of consummation. There is artistry in the selection of texts here which allows Colin to develop his theme in a full way without doing violence to, or leaving behind, the Scriptures on which he is preaching.

This is far from the only example. In the sermon on 'Ascension and Perfect Sacrifice', the Lukan ascension narrative is matched with a, perhaps obvious, ascension text from Hebrews, and a much less obvious temple text from Leviticus. Leviticus is allowed to create a context, a discussion of reality, and of the need for sacrifice, that makes sense of the Hebrews text, allowing it to be analysed on its own terms. And so the Gospel narrative, all but untouched in the sermon, is nonetheless illuminated. (This sermon also illustrates the skilful ways in which word and sacrament are tied together by Colin when he happened to be preaching on communion Sunday.)

III

I mentioned above the old idea of the 'analogy of faith' and hinted that it was relevant to understanding the way theology informs Bible interpretation and so preaching, as well as understanding how different passages of Scripture relate to each other. The argument went roughly like this: theology is assumed to be at heart no more than the ordered arrangement of the things taught plainly by Scripture, so when a particular text of Scripture is obscure or ambiguous, the teachings of theology can be invoked to explain it. Colin Gunton, of course, had a rather more nuanced account of the relation of theology to Scripture than is implied in this brief summary,[1] but he certainly believed that theology had a role to play in guiding the preacher in his or her approach to the Scriptures.

Reading through these sermons, it is striking that the (few) theological texts appealed to as authoritative are all widely agreed and authoritative statements of faith. This is obvious in the set of sermons on the Nicene Creed that Colin was in the midst of preaching when he died, but it also occurs elsewhere; we find reference made to the Heidelberg Catechism (Section

---

1 See, for instance, his essays on the nature of theology, 'A Rose by Any Other Name? From "Christian Doctrine" to "Systematic Theology"', *International Journal of Systematic Theology* 1(1) (1999): 4–23, or 'Historical and Systematic Theology', in C. Gunton (ed.) *The Cambridge Companion to Christian Doctrine* (Cambridge: Cambridge University Press, 1999), pp. 3–20.

Introduction

III of 'The Creed (1) Creation'), for instance. Not for Colin, however, the ostentatious display of learning so often heard in the pulpit, citing this or that theologian (almost always recent, and almost always second-rate) as if the authority of their genius settled the matter. Colin did not try to hide his learning; there are passing references to various theologians in many of these sermons. And the selection of authorities is largely unsurprising to someone who knew Colin's theological tastes: Irenaeus appears more than any other, with Calvin close behind, and Barth, Luther and the greatest of the Congregationalists, John Owen, being cited occasionally (Pusey appears once also, more surprisingly perhaps . . .). These great minds are not there, however, to foreclose discussion and still less are they called on to provide some sort of intellectual respectability that it is assumed the Scriptures lack. Rather they are simply illustrations: they are invoked, almost always, because they offer a striking and telling (Colin would have said 'lapidary') phrase that sums up a position. But that position is wrong, or in need of correction, almost as often as it is right, and there are as many or more lapidary quotations from the familiar hymnal as from the unfamiliar theological library. The Creeds and Confessions and, supremely, the Scriptures command our belief; the doctors merely our interest and engagement. I do not suppose for a moment that Colin planned his preaching to display such subtleties – which fact, assuming it is, makes the point all the stronger, that this was simply how Colin regarded the authorities.

I have remarked in print before now how much of Colin's theological work was carried on in community. That is in evidence in these sermons too. A chance conversation with a colleague and friend is the inspiration for preaching a series on the creed; a couple of conferences provide material to illustrate a point; two or three times the work of research students is noted as an illustration or a way into a theme. And, characteristically, Colin is always completely open about borrowing insights or ideas and completely original in his deployment of them. Although I think I can identify most or all of the unnamed conversation partners referred to in these sermons, it would perhaps not be proper to do so in print; I can confess to being both surprised and gratified, however, to discover that fifteen months into my own Ph.D. work with Colin it was being cited by him from the pulpit (in the first lines of the sermon on 'Eternal Punishment'). Of course, not every conference, conversation, or draft Ph.D. chapter was recycled into preaching matter, but there is a strong sense here that academic theology could and did sometimes provide the raw materials that were wanted for the church to be edified.

IV

What more to say? The sermons are characteristically Colin's: the tone of voice, the regular illustrations from art or literature or biography – even the odd joke about gardening! The language is always clear and careful, and one or two phrases are truly memorable: 'Napoleon and Hitler may both have failed in storming the gates of Moscow, but not McDonald's' ('Death and Modernity'); 'The resurrection is, to be sure, a mighty miracle, the miracle of all miracles. But it is the one who is raised that makes all the difference' ('The Resurrection and the Ascension'). The sermons are perhaps intellectual in their focus, more often exploring ideas than actions, theology than ethics, but always there is a clear conviction that right belief is necessary, if perhaps not sufficient (see the comments in the sermon on the Saint) to right action. Other preachers might perhaps want to be a bit more engaged with the world around: with one or two exceptions (9/11 being the most obvious), these sermons show little concern with agendas from news media or, indeed, any other media; and the turning of the Christian year is far more in evidence than the ephemeral events that capture the world's attention. The laconic comment '[e]ven if you leave the television off all or most of the time, as I do' ('Death and Modernity') is rather telling

Introduction

(although a humorous reference to the gardening programme *Ground Force* in 'The Meaning of Love' perhaps suggests what the television showed in its brief bursts of activity).

I suspect, however, that even this neglect of the contemporary is deliberate, and indicative of Colin's beliefs about preaching. Relevance is not to be strived for, simply because the gospel is necessarily already relevant to all people. One of the great themes of these sermons, surely, is asking what is truly relevant. Much of what passes for 'relevance' in our preaching is simply a capitulation to a pagan value system (or, at best, a despairing admission that one's congregation has capitulated). Sport or celebrity or items of passing notice in the news media are endlessly recycled in the pulpit in the (surely mistaken!) belief that this will aid the preacher in being heard. Colin's preaching challenged such assumptions and practices. This is very clear, for instance, in the comparison of temple sacrifice and banking practice in the sermon 'Ascension and the Perfect Sacrifice': 'Reality is our relations to God and to one another', and so the strange events of temple are more real than money and the banking system.

Of course, matters of true moment, on any value system, do make the news agenda, but what makes them of true moment is perhaps not their particularities and, certainly, not their contemporariness, but instead the fact that they are just one more expression of the things we all knew mattered all along. The truly significant realities of life – hope, despair, love, death and so on – are present in abundance in these sermons, and are rightly ordered. Every death appears a tragedy, whether it makes the news or not. And the calling of the preacher is to announce that this appearance is false, to proclaim hope in the face of every death indifferently, however public or private it might have been. Through reading all these sermons together there is a quiet but effective witness that the Gospel will speak hope to any and to all and that the particular situations people find themselves in are perhaps not the most important thing to be analysed. The sure hope of the resurrection of the dead is enough a few days after 9/11, as it is in the face of many, far less public but, for those involved, equally painful, events. It may be held up, almost without distinction, to a people bombarded with television coverage of that terrible day ('The Problem of Evil'), and to a people who have lost an old and dear friend ('Death and Readiness', preached at a funeral service).

V

What, then, might be the vital thing a theologian loses when he or she has stopped preaching? Something, I think, like this. Theology, if it is the church's science, has as its end presenting people holy before God. That is what is meant by claiming it is directed to the maintenance, edification and extension of the church of Christ. To be sure, the work of the theologian is often enough in apparently speculative or ephemeral issues which seem to have little to do with this great task, but the firming of foundations, the correction of errors and the sharpening of concepts are all finally directed to this end. The theologian, then, needs somehow to have this end in mind, to be actively engaged in the edification and extension of the church. For the Reformed theologian, this will almost inevitably happen through preaching (for others the celebration of the mass, or the ministry of spiritual direction, might serve the same end). The theologian who does not preach is in danger of pursuing arguments for the sake of argument, rather than for the sake of the Gospel, in which case, something vital is necessarily lost.

The converse, incidentally, may be said of the preacher who has given up on theology – not on reading recent academic theology, although that might be symptomatic, but on thinking as clearly and as hard as he or she can about the great truths of the faith, their foundations in the Scriptures, their interrelatedness and their practical outworkings. Of course, there is always a temptation in Christian ministry to bypass such work, to look for the quick fix, the plug-and-play solution that has

Introduction

been tested in the fires of pragmatism rather than those of truth. Such a preacher would no doubt find Colin Gunton's sermons rather puzzling: there is little attempt to grab attention; there are no easy answers; there is a straightforwardness and honesty about the real problems of faith and life. And yet underlying it all is an unshakeable confidence and a cheerful optimism. The gift of theology to preaching is roots that run deep and draw up the life-giving water that alone can truly refresh the people of God.

There is at present something of an explosion of books on homiletics, the art and science of preaching. In America the 'new homiletic' has arisen, leading to a re-evaluation of (what were perceived as) traditional modes of preaching. In all of this there is much about gaining and retaining the interest of a congregation, much about the gap between the Bible and the (post)modern world and, too often, rather little about theology. The sermons in this book would not, I suppose, win many prizes judged against such standards. The expert homiletician will look in vain for any awareness of 'Lowry loops', 'plotted moves' or narrative preaching. This might be a fault, but it is not a grievous one. The preachers who worry about such things typically are 'star names' who almost always are faced with new hearers looking to have their ears tickled pleasantly. This was not the case for Colin in Brentwood. He had no need to commend himself, or to seize his hearers; they knew him, and he knew them. He offered them little that was fancy, but plain, honest fare that would nourish those prepared to take it. The sermons in this book do not demand attention, but they do deserve it. And that, surely, is a commendation more to be valued than any of the changing winds of fashion.

*This book is dedicated to Colin E. Gunton's grandchildren,
including the three that he never met,
and also to the son-in-law that he never met.*

THE SERMONS

1
The Creed (1)
Creation

In the beginning, God created the heavens and the earth.
(Gen. 1.1)

4 FEBRUARY 2001

Readings: Gen. 1.1–13; Rom. 4.16–25; Lk. 8.40–2, 49–56

I

A few weeks ago, I was at a conference on the Nicene Creed. Each of the speakers was asked to take one of the clauses and explore what it meant both when it was written and for now. And I said to one of my friends that perhaps it might be a good idea to preach a series of sermons taking the creed clause by clause. In the modern world, when there is so much rank ignorance about the Christian faith, it is particularly important for Christians to be informed about their faith and what it claims. I shall take it clause by clause, but not necessarily in the order in which they appear in the creed. Today's subject was suggested by the new URC order for communion which we have been trying out in church recently. I commented to Robert[1] the other Sunday that it was inadequate in certainly one respect. Speaking of the creation, it speaks of God 'making order out of chaos'. Now, the second verse of Genesis' great chapter on creation might seem to justify that account of creation. 'The earth was without form and void,

---
1 Robert Canham, the then minister of Brentwood URC.

and darkness was upon the face of the deep.' It seems as though God is faced with Chaos, with something already there, and, through his Spirit, imposes order upon it.

Yet the classical Christian creeds are more radical than that. The Nicene Creed describes God as 'maker of heaven and earth'. The suggestion of that is that God is not like a potter who forms a shapeless piece of clay into a pot. He is the creator of all, clay and pot alike. 'Maker of heaven and earth'; again and again God is so described in Scripture, perhaps especially in the Psalms but elsewhere also. So, in that light, let us look at the first verse of Genesis' account of creation. 'In the beginning, God created the heavens and the earth.' This does not suggest that God comes upon a disordered world and then shapes it. He created everything. He is absolutely sovereign, the Lord who sits in the heavens and laughs at the absurd attempts of feeble man to displace him from his throne.

That means that in the light of Scripture as a whole, we have to say two things about the first chapter of Genesis. The first is that it shows, as we have already seen, God's sheer power and might. As we read through this wonderful chapter, with the spacious movement of the six days, beginning with light and ending with man, we see a sovereign creator at work, one who calls things into being with his word, shapes them and enables them in their turn to create new realities: 'let the earth bring forth living creatures'. Just think of the variety of ways God creates in that chapter, and you will realize what an astonishing passage it is, quite unique in the history of literature. This is a God known nowhere else.

The second point about the passage, however, is that it is not enough on its own for a fully Christian account of creation. For that we need Jesus also, to provide a lens through which to view Genesis. And in particular we need his resurrection. Let us pause to examine that for a while, and then return to the first verse of Genesis. In Romans, Paul speaks of 'the God who gives life to the dead and calls into being the things that are not'. In that chapter, he is in point of fact talking about God's having given a child to Abraham and Sarah when they were old, an act of power which was central to the Old Testament story. But it is also a clear reference to the resurrection of Jesus: 'who gives life to the dead'. One who can do that, who can transform a dead corpse into one who will live for ever, has all the power in the world. And so Paul adds: 'and calls into being the things that are not'. The resurrection of Jesus demonstrates God's sovereign power in action. In its light, Genesis is shown not to be an ancient myth, but the truth about the fact that it is the God of Israel and Jesus who calls the world into being and guides its course through time. In that light, then, let us turn to our text.

II

'In the beginning, God created the heavens and the earth.' The first point to be made is that this verse, according to the best recent scholarship, stands as a summary description of the whole chapter. Heaven and earth in Hebrew and in other ancient accounts of creation means simply 'everything'. And 'in the beginning' makes it clear that nothing begins without God's sovereign act. Once, there was nothing; and things began when God called them into being. 'In the beginning was the Word, and the Word was with God . . .'. Only through the eternal Word do things come to be. This is shown also by the word that Genesis uses here for created. When the author said that God 'created', he is using a Hebrew word used uniquely of God's creating act. We use the same word for all kinds of acts of creation: people create a garden, a mess, a meal. But this act, this act of creating everything in the beginning is uniquely God's. Everybody else has limits. A potter is limited by the qualities of the clay, a gardener by the conditions which can be changed, but only marginally. God is limited by nothing, for he is the God who creates by his sovereign word.

Let us now move to another detail of our text, where our author uses the expression 'heaven and earth'. What he means by earth is fairly obvious, but what of 'heaven'? It is not simply a place up there. In much of the biblical writing, and very likely in the background to Genesis, it may simply mean the literal heavens, the sky above; what the hymn calls the spacious firmament on high. The Genesis account is clothed in an ancient view of things that we no longer share, with water all around and a great dish placed over the earth to prevent it breaking in and drowning everything. But the biblical writers know very well that it is only a clothing for something far greater. Heaven is not for them limited to the sky, to the firmament of the ancient picture. Remember Solomon's prayer at the dedication of the temple: 'Behold, heaven and the heaven of heavens cannot contain thee; how much less this house which I have made . . .' (1 Kgs 8.27). God's creation far transcends the earth, and heaven is the word to describe that realm beyond.

The first thing we must learn from this is that God's creation is by no means limited to what we can see and touch. Another clause of the creed reminds us of this: 'and of all things visible and invisible'. 'There are more things in heaven and earth than are dreamt of in your philosophy . . .'.[2] Part of the poverty of our modern world is that it assumes that what you can see and hear, touch and taste and smell is all that there is. We are a materialist civilization whose imagination is limited to what happens to and in the human body – which means that we don't really have much imagination at all. When the shopping mall replaces the cathedral as the focus of our lives, we are in a poor way indeed. Rod[3] was telling me the other day that in poverty-stricken Russia great cathedrals are being built to replace those destroyed by the tyrannical materialists who once ruled there. That reminds us that heaven is a realm which transcends this one, something which is part of God's creation

---

2   *Hamlet*, Act I, Scene 5, Line 166–7.
3   Rod Cole, member of Dry Street Church where Colin Gunton preached regularly and Sarah Gunton's history teacher.

but whose reality we can barely glimpse. When we worship Sunday by Sunday, we are joined by angels and archangels and all the company of heaven, who join our praise with that of all God's creatures: that is something of what is meant by the heavenly realm.

And that takes me to a second point. 'Our Father, who art in heaven.' There is a sense in which God has his own place, his own base of operations, we might say, for his action in the world. In other words, heaven is not just another realm, but one from which our world is ruled. We should not misunderstand this. The story is often told of Khrushchev's glorying in the fact that the first man in space had not seen God when he was up there. That is just silly, for the very point is that heaven is not the same kind of place as ours, not our time and space but a realm encompassing and embracing ours. I like to tell to the children the story of Elisha and his young servant, surrounded as they are by enemy troops. So Elisha asks for the young man's eyes to be opened: 'and behold, the mountain was full of horses and chariots of fire round about Elisha' (2 Kgs 6.17). Recently some of my students presented me with an icon of Christ in glory,[4] and whatever we in our tradition are to make of icons, we can surely learn from them one thing: that Jesus of Nazareth, a man like us, is also the presence of the heavenly eternal and infinite world on earth, the kingdom of heaven in action among us. Heaven is God's realm, but is all about us because it is part of his one creation, the heaven and earth which he made in the beginning and continues to rule in his providential and merciful care.

In sum, heaven belongs with earth as part of God's world, yet as the place we cannot manipulate, a place of mystery that shows us that there is more to our world than we can know or think. And the earth, the second word used here, belongs within the overarching meaning provided by the heavens, because God reigns there, to redeem and to bless the world he

---

4   Also mentioned in the sermon preached on 23 September 2001.

loves so much that he sent his Son to become part of it. Perhaps the best illustration of this is to be found in the Book of Revelation, where the author shows us a battle going on in heaven, a battle in which the crucified Jesus overcomes the forces of darkness. That victory both encompasses and empowers the struggle of the martyrs as they live in a world given up to a great and materialistic empire like that in which we live. And that leads me to some of the things that the confession of God, the creator of heaven and earth, teaches us about our daily lives and struggles on earth.

III

One of the great Reformed confessions of faith, the Heidelberg Catechism, asks the following questions of the Lord's Prayer. 'Why is there added: "Who art in heaven"?' And it replies: 'That we may have no earthly conception of the heavenly majesty of God, but that we may expect from his almighty power all things that are needed for body and soul'. That there are heavens and that God reigns there reminds us that God is mysterious beyond our understanding, powerful and mighty as the one who raised Jesus from the dead. But that the heavens are part of his creation, part of God's world, means that our life on earth has a framework. It is not simply a world that gives us birth and kills us at the end of it. The earth on which we live is part of a wider order, a providential order set in place and maintained by the God and Father of our Lord Jesus Christ.

For us, this means two things in particular. First is that we must be conscious of where we come from and who holds us in being from day to day. I remember my friend Christoph Schwöbel commenting that it is important that at the beginning of every service of worship we should thank God for our creation, that we come out of nothing and only remain in being so long as God holds us there. We are completely and utterly dependent upon the God who made the heavens, the

The Creed (1) Creation

earth and all their furniture. This involves facing the fact that we are fragile creatures, made of the dust of the earth, and that we must die, for we live only so long as God wills. We have been aware of this in our church over recent weeks, with the various ills that have afflicted our members. It does no harm to remember, all of us, from time to time, that we come out of nothing, and will, apart from God's goodness, return to it.

And the reason that it does no harm to remember that we are mortal brings me to my second point, which is that we are created out of nothing by the one who raised Jesus from the dead: 'Underneath are the everlasting arms'. Our lives are indeed fragile and we move inexorably towards death. But we move there in a world ruled by the sovereign creator who raised from the dead our Lord Jesus Christ, and will in his own time give eternal life to our mortal bodies also.

2

The Creed (2)
Belief and the Role of the Church

I do believe. Help me overcome my unbelief.

(Mk 9.24)

2 MARCH 2003

Readings: 2 Kgs 6.8–17; Heb. 11.1–10; Mk 9.14–29; Ps. 18

I

We supposedly live in an age when belief is difficult, at least traditional Christian belief. That is what it is to be what is called 'modern', or modern western, we should more accurately say. Yet we should not suppose that there was ever a time when people did not have problems with the faith. Christian belief has always been difficult, offensive, because in all times and places it is difficult to believe that the outcome of our lives depends upon the fact that a young Jewish man once died on a cross; actually, it is not so much difficult as impossible, unless God should, through his Spirit, show us how things really are. It is thus that Paul speaks of the foolishness of the preaching of the cross. But we should remember that even within the world of faith the situation is a complex one, for in the Scriptures there is presented a whole range of responses to God and his word which show that human nature does not change that much. There have always been difficulties and differences over the Gospel and its acceptance, just as the story of Israel presents a wonderful panorama of different responses to God.

So far as faith or belief is concerned, we have in Scripture what appear to be two extremes, or, perhaps better, two poles or ends of the spectrum. The first appears in the account we heard of the disciples' failure to heal the son of the man who sought their help. Here we meet a man struggling with doubt. He had good reason. Jesus' disciples had sought to heal his epileptic son, and had failed. In response to the father's appeal for help, Jesus says, 'Everything is possible for him who believes'. And the man's reply is famous and forms our text, or at least one of the two I want to look at today. 'Lord I believe; help thou my unbelief', or, in the more clumsy but more modern way of putting it, 'I do believe. Help me overcome my unbelief'. The man is torn between two poles, just where we so often are. He believes, but there is a part of him which cannot be quite confident.

The apparent other end of the spectrum is illustrated by our reading from Hebrews: 'Faith gives substance to our hopes, and convinces us of realities we do not see' (Heb. 11.1). To see the point of the Letter to the Hebrews' confident account of what faith is, we have to remember that he is not giving a definition of faith; that is not, on the whole, the way Scripture works. Rather, he is telling of one of the things that faith does. The author wants here to celebrate the substance of faith; the fact that it really does deliver something. And there are at least two areas where he shows it to operate: in belief ('by faith we understand that the universe was formed by God's command') and in action ('by faith the walls of Jericho were made to fall'). Mostly, in fact, the chapter is a catalogue of things achieved through faith.

Are the two accounts not quite different? In the one case, believing against unbelief, and in the latter a calm confidence that faith delivers – delivers confidence because it is shown to work in a number of ways. In point of fact, I don't think that the poles are so far apart, especially if we remember that we should not treat the father in the story as an anxiety-torn modern. The point we need to hold in mind is that faith is a kind of personal relation, to God. In the end, faith is a form of trust. We trust all kinds of people, and yet the trust is never absolute. I remember that Jonathan was, when he was very small, quite happy for me to throw him in the air, pretend to drop him, and all the other things we do with small children. But if I held him off the ground near water – I remember an incident on Waterloo Bridge – he was stricken with panic. That is what our human condition is, whether it is directed to God or to another human being we know and trust. Lord, I believe. Help thou my unbelief. We know there are limits to our knowledge, courage and confidence. As the story of Jesus in the Garden of Gethsemane shows, there were times when his confidence was tested, to, though not beyond, its limits. And what he did there is the key to the matter, as is shown by the words with which Jesus caps the episode. 'This kind can come out only by prayer.' What does he mean by that? It is not, I think, that it is a matter of trying harder. It comes back to the matter of faith: that it is in prayer that we throw ourselves back on someone else's resources - or rather on God's, because they are the only ones which are adequate to the task. That is what happened both here and in Gethsemane. And it happens in life. I've been reading recently a book by a Jewish psychiatrist who has much to say about the nature and the healing of addiction. The most successful treatments, as with alcoholism, for example, are those that call upon the grace and power of God to do what is often humanly impossible. I think that is what Jesus means here. These can only be healed when you depend upon nothing but the power of God for which you can only pray.

II

Today's clause from the creed, as could have been predicted from the shape of things so far, is its opening two words: 'We believe'. When the church says, 'we believe', it is doing something similar to what it does when it prays. It is putting itself in a certain relation to God. And it is doing it as the church. Notice the 'we'. The later Apostles' Creed, as it is misleadingly called, says 'I believe', and that is far less satisfactory, because we, the church, can believe much more easily than the individual.

Let me try to explain something of the point of this. It is easy to treat the creed, especially in our age of apparent scepticism, as a list of things of which we might accept some of the more apparently credible but not others. It was said of some sceptical Oxford don that his limit was 'suffered under Pontius Pilate'. But many today will say things like, I can accept the resurrection at a pinch, but not the virgin birth, or the resurrection as long as it does not imply the actual restoration to life of an actual corpse. We can sympathize with those who take that kind of approach, for we live in a culture where sceptical arguments have affected people in that way through what are called the corrosions of modernity. Yet is it a mistake to see the creed as primarily a list of examinations, with some accepting only the easier questions, some tackling the harder. Christian faith is not a kind of assault course, and that is why the analogy of confessing the creed with prayer is illuminating and should always be kept in mind.

In prayer, it is not wrong to bring our lists of needs to God, to name before him, for example, those we care for and who are in need of his aid. But it is not the first thing about prayer, which is responding to God's goodness by putting ourselves freely in a certain position before him, as his creatures who cannot be truly ourselves without him. Of course we are going to have difficulties about some of the things confessed in the creed, partly because we do not always understand what they mean. I've spent most of my life trying to do that, and still find endless things to explore. But we also have doubts about some of those we do think we understand.

But that is not the main point, which is that it is not *my* but *our* faith that we confess. Calvin said that when we confess, 'We believe in one holy, catholic and apostolic church', it does not mean that we believe *in* it as we believe in God, but that we believe *it*, have confidence in its teaching and message. That may be right or wrong, but it makes a point. We do not do this as individuals but as members of a great community of belief, and we are entrusting ourselves to its traditions and its confidence in God. This is a community that has outlived all kinds of threats and ideologies, has stood firm in the face of persecution, right up to those recent ones by Nazism and Communism, and has continued to grow in extent and numbers throughout its history. Despite centuries of hostile propaganda, it seems that a majority of British people, and especially in Brentwood, still call themselves Christian, however little it may sometimes mean – though that is not for us to judge. We are surrounded by a great cloud of witnesses, looking to and pointing us to the Lord who died on the cross.

Where Calvin is wrong is that there is a sense in which we do believe in the church, because by joining it we commit ourselves to fellowship with all those millions of people through time and space. We can confidently say the things that they have so long said and continue to say, because we trust God through them. I think that is part of what is meant by Jesus' promise to Peter, that the gates of hell will not prevail against the church. Our confidence is primarily in God, but secondarily and yet truly in the people he has given us to share our pilgrimage.

'I do believe. Help me overcome my unbelief.' That is true of us all in different ways. But the dominating truth is that God has given us help for our unbelief, as through his Son he did for that sick boy what his father asked. 'Faith gives substance to our hopes, and convinces us of realities we do not see.' The reason why we do have our doubts and fears and anxieties is that we do not yet see, but live, by faith. But faith is not a second-rank substitute for something better. It is the only way for those who are still on the way to the time when God will be all in all. Faith is not hanging on despite the evidence; quite the reverse. It is depending on the plentiful evidence that we do have and remembering that it is not for us to see the distant scene. As our text says, it gives substance to our hopes, assures us that they are not empty hopes. Living by faith is living in the only way limited and sinful creatures may do. But it is a way with substance. And the reason is given us in the creed. The eternal Son of God became man for us, and shared our testing, as we have seen, to the very limit of his endurance. And he was enabled to endure because he was upheld in his relation to his Father by that very Spirit who upholds us also on our way through life. Faith gives real substance because it is commitment to a person or, rather, to God the Father of our Lord Jesus Christ through his Spirit – to one person through two others. And that is why the creed has the form it has: we believe in one God, the Father, maker of heaven and earth; and in one Lord Jesus Christ; and in the Holy Spirit, the Lord, the giver of life.

The Spirit gives us life, life in relation to God the Father who loved us so much that he sent his only Son to die for us. Like all life on earth, it is a fragile thing, subject to weakness and sickness, and, sometimes, to being taken away by others. And yet it is life, with substance, because it is the gift of God, convincing us of realities we do not yet see.

III

As I said at the beginning, we are modern people and, therefore, tend to have more difficulty than most ages of history with Christian belief, though not with believing many things that later generations will no doubt come to find quaint if not absurd. The explosion of Christian conversions and martyrdoms in places like China should remind us, however, that it is we in the West who are unusual, not those who believe in their millions. As we have seen, the point of confessing the creed is several-fold. Among the first, however, is the *we*: that in our believing in God we join ourselves to a great tradition of believers who have seen off one threat to the Gospel after another. With them, we believe, committing ourselves week by week and day by day to the God who loves us for ever, through and despite our weakness, until the day when we shall truly know as we are known.

3

The Creed (3)
God's Covenant

> For this reason Christ is the mediator of a new covenant, that those who are called may receive the promised eternal inheritance . . .
>
> (Heb. 9.15)

BRENTWOOD COVENANT SERVICE, 12 JANUARY 2003

Readings: Heb. 9.11–15, 24–8; Mk 14.17–25

I

These days, it is gift aid; once it was covenants, and the fact that the word 'covenant' was used shows that the language of Scripture has found its way into the language of modern finance. Those covenants were promises to pay money to a charity. They were not enforceable in law, so that if you became bankrupt or moved to another church, or simply just gave up on it, there was no penalty. That is where a covenant is different from a contract. If you make a contract with a builder, and either he fails to do what he agrees or you fail to pay him, there will be penalties enforceable at law. Thus there is a freedom about a covenant that does not apply to a contract. That brings out for us one of the meanings of covenant in its original, biblical setting: it is simply a free gift from God, unmerited, gracious, loving. God did not have to promise not to inundate the world again after the flood. A cautious operator would have said – if you do it again, the sentence next time will be worse – prison for a second offence, so to speak. But God is not a cautious operator, as the very existence of the covenants shows.

Similarly, God did not have to choose Israel from among the nations. He could have chosen a much more attractive bride, like a Jane Austen suitor after beauty and a fortune to match. 'The Lord did not set his affection on you and choose you because you were more numerous than other peoples . . . But it was because the Lord loved you' (Deut. 7.7f). And what happened when Israel regularly broke the promises she made in response? Through Jeremiah, God promised a new covenant: 'I will put my law in their minds, and write it on their hearts. I will be their God, and they will be my people' (Jer. 31). And that is but a selection of the things called covenants in the Old Testament. We could add the covenant with Abraham, with which God begins to build again after the disaster of the fall and all that happened from there to Babel, and the covenant with David.

Every one of the ancient covenants was fulfilled in Jesus. But I am going too fast. Before coming to him, and to our text, there is one more thing that has to be said. Covenants are indeed free gifts of God. They are indeed one-sided, to the extent that he gives, and his people can but receive. But they are not entirely one-sided. They bring obligations. Abraham has to leave his home; Israel is expected to obey the law, to care for the widow, orphan and stranger, to live honourably in the land God gives them. And despite the promise that the flood will not be repeated, there are consequences to the breach of covenant. God is gracious, merciful and forgiving, but he is also holy and is not mocked. He is a loving but also stern father. Corrupt kings and the grinding of the poor still bring their consequences. The kings fall and Israel goes into exile. Covenants are free gifts, but they do not represent endless indulgence, for we know what happens to children who are completely spoiled.

II

And so we come to our text. 'For this reason Christ is the mediator of a new covenant, that those who are called may receive the promised eternal inheritance' (Heb. 9.14). For this reason. Our writer is comparing and contrasting the old covenant, as that was seen in Israel's sacrificial system, and the new. He does not deny that the old covenant worked but claims that it does not truly reach the heart. The blood of goats and bulls, he says, makes people outwardly clean; but this covenant is the fulfilment of Jeremiah's promise of a new covenant, according to which God will write his law not on tablets of stone, but on human hearts: 'cleansing our consciences from dead works, so that we can serve the living God'.

There is in these chapters of Hebrews a running contrast between what the high priest did, and what Jesus has done. The priest had to perform sacrifices regularly; Jesus made one of himself. The priest went into a merely man-made sanctuary; Jesus went to the heavenly sanctuary, and so on. The contrast enables our author to expound the two central aspects of the achievement of Jesus. The first concerns his death, and for that our author has two words: it is a ransom, and it is a sacrifice. Both are pictures, metaphors which bring out different aspects of the truth of the Gospel. The ransom is the money a father or uncle paid to recover a soldier taken prisoner in war and otherwise condemned to slavery. It is a way of speaking of God's covenanted generosity. We fall into slavery, by our own stupid fault; he stumps up the money to set us free. The sacrifice – 'by the sacrifice of himself' – on the other hand, is an even more central image, for it concerns self-giving. You can hardly make too much of this, according to our author. The death of Jesus on the cross is the self-giving to death of the one through whom the universe was made. It is therefore of eternal and universal significance, unique, unrepeatable, incomparable. It means that we live in a new era, the era of the new covenant: 'now he has appeared once for all at the end of the ages to do away with sin by making a sacrifice of himself'. So that is the first great contrast our author wants to make. The ancient priest had to perform repeated sacrifices. This one is both priest and sacrifice, and the sacrifice is of himself.

The second contrast between Jesus and the high priest concerns his ascension. We tend not to make a lot of ascension in the modern church, but for our author it is absolutely indispensable. Jesus, says Hebrews, did not merely go into a tent or a temple; he went into heaven itself – 'now to appear for us in God's presence'. Eternally before the throne of the Father, there is one who pleads our cause, the one through whom God views us, seeing not our sins and wickedness, but ourselves as we are, to use Calvin's phrase, clothed with Christ's righteousness. The one who died for us is eternally our advocate with the Father.

Isaac Watts brings together both of our themes, death and Christ's heavenly intercession, in a verse of a hymn:

> Jesus my great High-Priest, offered his blood and died:
> my guilty conscience seeks no sacrifice beside;
> his powerful blood did once atone, and now it pleads
>   before the throne.[1]

Each of those two events of Jesus' career, his death and his ascension, has something to say to us about what we are doing here. The death is the sealing of the covenant, the last and greatest of God's acts of sheer generosity to us who have made ourselves his enemies. That the Son of God should go to the cross for us shows at once the greatness of the need and the unfathomable generosity of the God who calls us to be his own. So we eat the bread and drink the cup, in memory of him to anchor ourselves to that event in which he underwent judgement for us, went armed only with the power of the

---

1 United Reformed Church, *Rejoice and Sing* (Oxford: Oxford University Press, 1991), 280.

Spirit into the fearsome realm of evil to conquer it and free us from its power. And the ascension reminds us that we do it 'until he comes'. We live in the new age, and yet we do not live in the new age. We live, in a famous expression, 'between the times': between his death and his coming again in glory to judge both the living and the dead. We live in the age of the greatest and best of the covenants, that in which God did not spare his own Son, but gave him up, so that we might live in newness of life.

Part of that 'newness of life' is living as if we mean it, learning to live according to the ways of the new world. And the covenant we today renew before God and with each other and, indeed, with all God's people, is one of the ways we do it. As God commits himself to us in this astonishing way, as Jesus represents us for ever before the throne of grace, so we commit ourselves to live in his light, to accept from him the resources that we need to live in his way, by the laws of his kingdom. God's covenantal love evokes in us the only adequate response: to offer ourselves, our souls and bodies, as a living sacrifice in his service.

III

One final point, as a kind of coda: God holds to his covenants but is not limited by them. That is the message of the story of his covenants from Noah and Abraham to the new covenant in the blood of Christ.

> Great is thy faithfulness, O God my Father,
> Morning by morning new mercies I see;
> all I have needed your hand has provided . . .[2]

---

2 *Rejoice and Sing*, 96. William Runyan William/Thomas O. Chisholm. Copyright © 1923, renewed 1951. Hope Publishing Company administered by Copycare, PO Box 77, Hailsham BN27 3EF, UK; music © copycare.com. Used by permission.

One of the great expressions in our language is 'uncovenanted blessings'. Just pause to think upon it. Blessings enough are covenanted, but out of his boundless generosity, God gives us yet more. No wonder then that we should, in the words sometimes used at this table, eat, drink and be thankful.

4

The Creed (4)
Normality and the Image of God[1]

> Look at my hands and my feet. It is I myself! Touch me and see;
> a ghost does not have flesh and bones, as you see I have.
>   (Lk 24.39–40)

THIRD SUNDAY OF EASTER, 4 MAY 2003

Readings: Acts 3.12–19; 1 Jn 3.1–7; Lk. 24.36–48

I

It might seem to be the case, but it is not, that we have an interest in or benefit from the rise of interest in what is known as the paranormal: the spooky realm. Bookshops are now full of it, but it is our foe, not our ally. If all that stuff is what religion involves, then we are not religious. What often goes under the name of 'spirit' or 'spiritual' is not about the Holy Spirit at all. Our concern is not for the paranormal but for the normal: not for another world, but for this one, the one the Lord created and has redeemed through the blood of his Son. In that light, let us look at two of the puzzles of the Gospel reading we have just heard.

The first concerns the nature of the body of the risen Lord. Two weeks ago we encountered something of the fact that the risen Jesus is often not recognized. Mary takes him for the gardener of Gethsemane. In Luke's account of what happens rather later in the day, there is a similar failure, with rather

---

1   The sermon preached by Colin Gunton two days before his death.

23

different effect. Jesus' appearance, apparently sudden, and his greeting shocks and startles them, and they thought he was a ghost. He tells them as he tells Thomas in the story in John, to look at his wounds and speaks the following highly significant words: 'touch me and see; a ghost does not have flesh and bones, as you see I have'. The lesson is hammered home by his eating fish in front of them. Luke is clearly making a point: this is a physical event – not a ghost but a resurrection of the flesh.

Yet it is a strange kind of physicality. He appears and disappears, and is at least rather like a ghost, apparently walking through closed doors. That is the puzzle of the resurrection: a man who is not easily recognized, who eats and goes through closed doors. I think the clue to it is given in C. S. Lewis's famous book, *The Great Divorce*. The hero goes on a bus journey to a place which we eventually know to be heaven, gets out of the bus, and he sees that as some of the passengers walk on the grass, it does not bend under their feet. He thinks they are ghosts.

> Then some re-adjustment of the mind or focusing of my eyes took place, and I saw the whole phenomenon the other way round. The men were as they had always been . . . It was the light, the grass, the trees that were different; made of some different substance, so much solider than things in our country that men were ghosts by comparison.[2]

Jesus is not a ghost; rather, he is more real than the doors and walls which cannot hold him in; not immaterial but more material, more substantial, more solid. The resurrection has given him a better, heavenly body, what Paul in 1 Corinthians calls a spiritual body – a body suffused by the Spirit of God, and so become what it was created to be. He is now not

---

[2] C. S. Lewis, *The Great Divorce* (London: HarperCollins, 2002), p. 21. Copyright © C. S. Lewis Pte Ltd, 1946. Extract reprinted by permission.

limited by space and time, but their Lord even more truly than when he healed the sick and raised the dead. But he is still of flesh and blood, can eat and be touched. The poet Gerard Manley Hopkins knew this well:

> Man's spirit will be flesh bound when found at best,
> But uncumberèd: meadow-down is not distressed
> For a rainbow footing it nor he for his bónes rísen[3]

Notice the wonderful image of the rainbow on that lightest of matter, meadow-down. So, he says, it is with the Lord; he is physical and free of many of the limitations of our fallen existence. Again, John has an interesting parallel in the story of Lazarus. Lazarus is resuscitated, brought back to his old life. As Jesus says, he will die again. Those who are raised from the dead in the way that Jesus is, the firstborn of many brothers and sisters, will not die again. That is what is meant by eternal life, the raising of our bodies to the conditions of the life to come.

That is our destiny. The end of our days is not to become ghosts, but to be transformed to be like him: to be really, finally human and fleshly, again like the figures in Lewis's vision of heaven.

> Some were naked, some robed. But the naked ones did not seem less adorned, and the robes did not disguise in those who wore them the massive grandeur of muscle and the radiant smoothness of flesh. Some were bearded but no one in that company struck me as being of any particular age. One gets glimpses, even in our country, of that which is ageless – heavy thought in the face of an infant, and frolic childhood in that of a very old man. Here it was all like that.[4]

---

3 Gerard Manley Hopkins, 'The Caged Skylark'.
4 C. S. Lewis, *Great Divorce*, p. 23, *op. cit.*

We are created to be perfected, to become what the Lord wishes us to be, like those people in the novel, joyful, loving and whole in every way. Our sin brings it about that this does not happen; indeed, with the whole earth we share a rather opposite destiny, death, dissolution, a return to the nothingness from which we came. The resurrection shows us that what Jesus achieved on the cross has broken the power of death, broken our helter-skelter rush to ruin. The grace and love of God is such that he does not allow his holy one to see corruption, his world to sink into final decay. We must die, and the universe must eventually dissolve into utter heat or deathly cold. But the new heaven and the new earth not only await, but have begun in the resurrection of Jesus from the dead.

II

Let us now move to our other puzzle, a bit more briefly this time. In the same passage, Luke tells us – and it is not the only time he tells us in this chapter – that all this happens according to the Scriptures, that it is all written about in what we call the Old Testament. But it does not seem to be. There is a vision of the resurrection in Ezekiel 37, and the occasional reference to the third day – but nothing that would really count as a prediction. Why is the New Testament so confident that all is predicted? Well, what might that involve? It involves the promises of God, not the particular means of their fulfilment. The story that Scripture tells is one of creation, fall and redemption. God creates a good world and places his human creatures in it. Inexplicably, they fall; they turn back to destruction rather than forward to the fulfilment God offers those who walk in his ways. And the story from then on is forever renewed promises of redemption: Abraham, Moses, Israel, the prophets – one after another, God calls people to be the mediators of his determination that his human creation shall be reconciled to him. The way in which the promise is renewed is always surprising, unpredictable in a straightforward sense, as is the coming and resurrection of Jesus. But seen backwards, so to speak, it is the obvious outcome. Read the Scriptures with Jesus in mind, and you will see that in them God prepares the way for him. There is another way in which the whole story can be told. God created the world through and for Christ, and that world is directed to him, as its destiny and purpose. What Jesus calls the Scriptures and we the Old Testament is, as a whole, a preparation for the one in whom all things will be summed up, all completed, all made what they were created to be. 'For no matter how many promises God has made, they are "Yes" in Christ' (2 Cor. 1.20). In his resurrection, we see the beginning of the end, the inexorable move towards the renewal of all things in Christ and through the Spirit.

III

I have, as you know, been taking month by month clauses from the Nicene Creed, and it could be said that today have but touched on a number, albeit in a rather general way. The chief ones concern the utter physical concreteness of the events of Good Friday and Easter: 'crucified . . . buried . . . rose on the third day'. The second is, as you will have realized, 'according to the Scriptures'. This is the Lord's work, and it marks the unfathomability and sheer wonder of his grace: that not only did the Son of God take flesh and suffer for our sakes, but that God prepared the way for him in such a way that we should be able to grasp something of the significance of these astonishing events.

What the puzzles I have explored bring home to us is the nature of the creed and of our belief. It is confession, not philosophical certainty. But it does have a kind of certitude, something we can hang our eternal salvation on, because it makes sense of ourselves and our world. On Friday I was at a conference devoted to the thought of the philosopher of science, Michael Polanyi, who argued that all our beliefs, including those of the scientist, are personal. Nothing is absolutely objective, because we do not have a Godlike view of things, only one that is limited by – yes, that again – our human fleshliness. Polanyi has a wonderful slogan, which is worth repeating, and, indeed, learning. He tells us that we have to develop a frame of mind: 'in which I may hold firmly to what I believe to be true, even though I know that it may conceivably be false'. Anything we say or believe may conceivably be false. I know of someone who lost her faith through constantly subjecting it to doubt – could it be false? – and she came to convince herself that it was. The fact is that you can convince or unconvince yourself of many things if you try hard enough. That is why we confess the creed, not to convince ourselves – only the Spirit can do that – but to remind ourselves of the things that make for true life. We confess the creed in confidence that God has indeed raised Jesus from the dead, the first-fruits of the final kingdom.

> In hope, against all human hope, self-desperate, I believe;
> thy quickening word shall raise me up, thou shalt thy
>   Spirit give.[5]

Notice the 'self-desperate'. We are the problem, not the things we believe.

We confess the creed in confidence. That does not mean that everything is made as clear as day. These things are mysteries, because there is always more to be gained from them. But they are not mysteries meant to baffle or to take us out of this world into the realm of the paranormal. The mysteries show us what normality is, which is, I think, why the epistle reading, that from the first letter of John, was placed alongside the others in today's lections. It is to do with normality in two ways. First, that we have through all this been made God's

---

5 *Rejoice and Sing*, 351.

children, and that means that we have to behave as though we are. John's letter is written in part to urge on his friends the fact that because they have been loved, then they should love one another. This is the most normal and concrete matter of all: getting on with your neighbour, especially in the fellowship of the church.

The second is in the mysterious promise, that when Jesus appears a second time, 'we shall be like him, for we shall see him as he is'. We shall be like him: that is normality. Our human calling – normality – is to be in the image of God. We fail in our calling, but in his wonderful grace he calls us to be his children. To be like him, like the one who rose on Easter morning, is to be made like him, truly the people we were created to be. This is not about magic, not about ghosts; but about the way the Lord providentially and graciously tends his creation and restores us to and holds us in his love.

5
Prophets and Apostles

See, I will send my messenger, who will prepare the way before me. Then suddenly the Lord you are seeking will come to his temple.

(Mal. 3.1)

PALM SUNDAY, 24 MARCH 2002

Readings: Mal. 3.1–5; 1 Cor. 9.1–14; Mk 11.1–11

I

'Blessed is the kingdom of our father David which is coming', cried the crowds according to Mark's account of what we call Palm Sunday. What went on in Jerusalem about the time of the death of Jesus had an air of expectation about it, perhaps of some Messianic demonstration, perhaps of the Lord's final victory over the enemies of Israel. Very likely for some the end really was imminent. There were plenty of apocalyptic prophets around at that time to promise it, Barabbas possibly among them. Well, it was the end. Let me simply list some of the events as Mark records them. Our reading ends rather ominously, 'He entered Jerusalem and went into the temple. He looked round at everything: then, as it was already late, he went out to Bethany'. The next day he curses a fig tree, cleanses the temple, and, on his return, finds the fig tree, symbol of Jerusalem, withered and dead. Then parables of judgement, political conflict, the prophecy of the end, and his own death. Some of us have recently heard on our tapes the story as Mark tells it. It is replete with conflict, ominous with doom and ends with the event which seals the fate of the great city, destined as it was to be destroyed by the Romans.

The prophet Malachi wrote, 'See, I will send my messenger, who will prepare the way before me. Then suddenly the Lord you are seeking will come to his temple'. Well, suddenly the Lord did come to his temple, in the one violent act told of him, in the wrath of divine judgement. Here, the one who comes to the temple is both messenger and Lord, but he is accepted in neither role. He is indeed the messenger who is sent by the Father; but as the Son who does the Father's work, he is also the Lord God in person claiming the temple which had become corrupt and calling down judgement on the city which had abandoned its calling, an abandonment it would prove by, as they say, shooting the messenger.

Malachi means 'messenger', and it may be that this prophet got his name because of this famous line in his short book. This is the last book in the Old Testament canon – for Christians the final messenger before the two great gospel messengers, John the Baptist and Jesus himself. And Malachi is the last of a very long line, beginning with Moses and including a long list of prophets. Often the messengers whom God sends resist his call, either because they do not want to serve or because they feel themselves unworthy. But God will not accept 'no' for an answer. (I'm always made uneasy by the hymn we sometimes sing, though not by my choice, when we thank God for letting us answer 'yes' or 'no'. We can, I think, be glad that when God wants something done, he will not take 'no' for an answer, or, indeed, let us escape the duty and delight which is God's call to us.)

Sending messengers is God's way of getting things done. In Mark 12, the chapter after the description of the Palm Sunday entry into Jerusalem, Jesus tells the parable of the vineyard owner who sends one messenger after another to his corrupt and murderous tenants, until finally he sends his son, whom they murder. The message is clear: God sends a series of messengers, including his own Son, and they are rejected. And yet, the message of Palm Sunday and its outcome is also clear. This messenger is the Lord himself, who comes in person to see that things are done as his Father wishes, and his very death, far from being the end of his mission, is his glorious coronation as not only prophet, but our priest and king also. 'See, I will send my messenger, who will prepare the way before me. Then suddenly the Lord you are seeking will come to his temple.'

II

As we have seen, in the Old Testament, the messengers to whom God's very words are entrusted are his prophets, those who stand in his council and hear the very words they are to speak. 'Thus says the Lord; this is the very word of God.' In the New Testament, the equivalent is the apostle. Indeed, the two groups, prophets and apostles, are so at the heart of things that if you say, 'the prophets and apostles', that is one way of speaking of the writers of the Old and New Testaments. In their persons and their offices they sum up what the writers of these books mean to us, because they are central among the messengers of God. The prophets are those who prepare the way for the coming of the Lord to his temple; the apostles those who tell us why and how it happened, for our conversion and edification.

Let me today, however, look at the second group in particular. 'Apostle' simply means one who is sent. First of all in the New Testament the word refers to the twelve, those who were witnesses of the resurrection. That is why Paul made the claim that he, also, is an apostle. 'Am I not an apostle? Have I not seen Jesus our Lord?' He is *our* apostle, for he believed that it was his particular apostolate to preach the Gospel to the Gentiles. We are here because of the message Paul was charged with. It may, indeed, be the case that Paul believed that he was the twelfth, the one called to make up the number after the death of Judas, and it is certainly true that we hear nothing after his election of the one chosen according to Acts to make up the number of twelve.

Be that as it may, 'apostle' is used in the New Testament more broadly than just of the twelve. Others are given that title, and that is important for our purposes, when we speak of the church, the church which we are, as 'apostolic'. The word is used quite generally of those who had been called by God to serve the gospel. My own teacher used to annoy the high churchmen by suggesting that the person named as an apostle in Romans 16.7, which could be either a masculine or feminine form in the Greek, was probably a woman. (NIV: 'Junias'; Revised English Bible, 'Junia'.) We cannot tell for certain, but it is clear that 'apostle' was used generally of those who were sent, entrusted with a message or task from God. It is a Greek word, and the Latin equivalent is the word that gives us 'mission'. A mission is something you are sent to perform, anything, that is, that God sends us to do. So, for Scripture, the apostles are the first to be sent to witness to the resurrection of Jesus. They are special because they are the first. But they are not alone. All those who hear the call to be members of the body of Christ are sent to do the same: to witness in their own particular way to the fact that they – we – have been sent. The whole church is in that sense 'apostolic', sent by God into the world that he has loved for the sake of that world, so that all may ultimately be reconciled to their maker and live in peace on his good earth. We believe in one holy, catholic 'and apostolic church'.

III

What does it mean to say that the church is apostolic? First, it is founded on the witness of the prophets who looked forward to Christ and the apostles who saw and knew the risen Christ. The prophets and apostles are the bedrock on which all other prophecy and apostolicity rest. They are the ones who have foreseen and seen the Lord, who show us what it means that he came and will come again to his temple, the next time in glory to complete the judgement he began at Jerusalem. As

Paul writes to the Ephesians, 'You are built on the foundation of the prophets and apostles, with Christ Jesus himself as the corner-stone' (Eph. 2.20). Forget that, and the whole is lost.

But there is a second also important sense of 'apostolic'. The church is apostolic in being sent out into God's world. In that respect, the whole church is, after the prophets and apostles, apostolic. Different churches have different ways of organizing this, from the more Catholic churches who claim that their apostolicity comes down through the bishops, to the churches of the Reformation who trace it to the tradition of teaching, whether through bishops or anyone else. In our church, an important part of our way of being apostolic – of realizing the fact that we are sent on a mission – is through the office of elder. Elders are as crucial to the life of the church as ministers – perhaps in some respects more so, because the church can cope without a minister, but not without those who hold together the pastoral life of the church all the time. If I or any other minister were from this pulpit or in any other way to do things which undermine the worship and life of this church, it would be their duty to reprove or even see to my removal. That, of course, is the negative side. Positively, there is the constant caring for the life of the church and the pastoral care of the sick and needy.

'See, I will send my messenger, who will prepare the way before me. Then suddenly the Lord you are seeking will come to his temple.' We are the temple. Notice again the imagery of Ephesians: 'You are built on the foundation of the prophets and apostles, with Christ Jesus himself as the corner-stone'. We are like the stones of a great building and have to be built up, again and again, into a structure that witnesses to the great things God has done and, especially, to the resurrection of Jesus. As such, we are the city on the hill, the light shining into a dark and wicked world. We might say that the elders are to this building what the men's working group are to our premises. Without them, it would not immediately fall down, but would certainly fail to be what it is made to be. I notice that in a recent denominational circular for our district about 'natural church growth', one of the conditions for a growing church is dispersed leadership – leadership which is spread around. (I would actually prefer to say, dispersed ministry, because we are called to be ministers, not leaders, but let that go for now.)

'You are Peter, and on this rock I will build my church, and the gates of hell will not prevail against it.' That is the promise. We are built upon the witness of Peter and the other apostles, so that we become apostolic ourselves. Notice, however, who does the building in the first instance: the Lord who comes to his temple and will come again to complete what he has begun. In that promise, that the gates of hell will not prevail, we worship week by week, we elect our elders, and thank God that we have them.

6

The Worldly Christ

Therefore when Christ came into the world, he said: 'Sacrifice and offering you did not desire, but a body you prepared for me'.
(Heb. 10.5)

FOURTH SUNDAY IN ADVENT, 23 DECEMBER 2001

Readings: Lk. 1.26–38; 2 Sam. 7.1–11, 16; Heb. 10.5–10

I

Once more the marathon is almost at an end. There used to be a saying, that there were two things you could not avoid in this life, death and taxes. Recently, someone added a third: death, taxes and Christmas. I continue to enjoy it, largely because of this community and the whole church's celebration of what one journalist, I am sorry to say, called the Reincarnation. But there is something to be said for the view, I think put forward by the Archbishop of Westminster recently, that the thing has become so paganized that we might be better, as Christians, to abandon our celebration of it.

Well, has it been paganized, and what does that mean? I think that to be pagan is essentially to worship this world, and that means ultimately ourselves, rather than the great creator. There is plenty of evidence that this happens. Christmas represents in this respect the ultimate sin, the definition of sin, as worshipping the creature rather than the creator. And yet, and yet, as so often in this realm, we can so easily slip over into the opposite error of denying the fact that even this material earth which we so misuse is God's creation and given for our use and enjoyment. It is not part of Christian belief to devalue or reject the world; even orders of monks and nuns were founded for the sake of the world, not to escape it. How do we find the right measure in these matters?

'One Lord Jesus Christ . . . who . . . was incarnate by the Holy Spirit and the Virgin Mary, and was made man.' Here, in one part of the creed's confession of the Son of God, two real, flesh-and-blood human beings, Jesus and Mary, are mentioned; unusual human beings, it must be confessed, but true ones nevertheless. The creed makes clear that they are beings who belong to this world, like the rest of us. And here we meet the question for today. In the press, we have had news of the inevitable Christmas storm in a teacup: a cleric in Ireland has been suspended for saying that Jesus is only an ordinary human being like us.

The problem is not in the claim, but in the 'only'. One wonders what kind of world this man thinks he is living in. It is one torn apart by greed, suffering and, as we have seen these past few months, continuing bloodshed. Only God can deal with that. That is what this season is all about. Yet, and this is the other side of the same matter, he deals with it in a worldly way: he makes himself a house of clay. We do not worship the world – that is paganism – but we do confess a creed which is worldly in the best sense, about human life in the body and in this world of things. The key to it all is to be found in the two crucial figures mentioned in our clause: the Holy Spirit and the Virgin Mary. Let us look at them one at a time with the help of our text.

II

First, the Holy Spirit. 'Therefore, when Christ came into the world, he said: "Sacrifice and offering you did not desire, but a body you prepared for me"'. In point of fact, our author is rather mistranslating a psalm there, but it does not matter, for it is what he does with it that counts. He does share the psalmist's estimate of the human condition: it is no good slaughtering beasts or giving money to God when the real problem is the wickedness of the human heart. The heart, remember, is part of the human body: it is what makes us tick, in two senses, both physically and morally. And it is the second of those two respects – the heart as representing the kind of people that we are – that we are concerned with. Notice the way that we speak of people: they are hard-hearted, soft-hearted, good-hearted, tender-hearted, stony-hearted (a biblical image, that) and the rest. And the problem with it is that – apart from what God does with it – the heart is mortally sick, corrupting us – yes – to the very heart of our being. There is only one cure: a repairing of the human condition from within. And so God prepares a human body for his Son: 'a body you prepared for me'. That is the point about the creed's reference to the Holy Spirit. Here is the power of God at work renewing his creation – the world with which we have been concerned from the beginning of this sermon, the world which is worshipped and misused by our behaviour. Notice how in both Luke's and Matthew's accounts of this matter the action of the Spirit is so prominent: 'the Holy Spirit will come upon you, and the power of the Most High will overshadow you' (Lk. 1.35). Or Matthew: 'what is conceived in her is from the Holy Spirit' (Mt. 1.20).

Our salvation begins with a miracle, something wonderful beyond our imagining. The power of his Spirit, by whom God rules all his world, is here concentrated at this particular point, this time of our history. Through his Spirit, God, so to speak, homes in on one place in his world for the sake of the whole. 'When the time was right, God sent forth his Son' – and in a body prepared for him by this particular act of the Spirit. Through the act of his creator Spirit, the Lord acts to renew the creation from within, having prepared the way through his people Israel, as one of whom this child is born. The one who hovered over the waters of creation hovers over this young girl in a new and miraculous act of the Spirit, where God begins to recreate his lost world.

Second: 'By . . . the Virgin Mary'. The doctrine of the virgin birth of Jesus has often been used as a kind of proof of the divinity of Jesus, but it is a mistake to see it mainly in that way. In one respect, that is certainly the case. By showing that he does not need a man in this process – and notice the NIV rendering of John 1.13: 'not . . . of human decision or a husband's will' – God demonstrates his power and sovereignty. This is a new, re-creative act by the Spirit – as we have seen, a miraculous new beginning which only God can achieve. But in another respect, quite the opposite point is intended. The doctrine of the virgin birth is just as much about the kind of human being that Jesus is. It is, again, about the worldly way in which our God acts. It is about a new and redeemed humanity, the second Adam come to reverse the false step taken by the first. What is the problem? It is what the hymn calls 'this weary, soiled earth'. By the power of his Spirit, God takes ordinary human genetic material, from an ordinary girl of flesh and blood.[1] The key to the matter is Mary's ordinariness, the ordinariness that makes her the first and representative Christian, the one who simply – like Abraham before her – does the bidding of her Lord. Mary's genetic inheritance is like ours; soiled and corrupted by centuries of human fault. And through the power of his Spirit God cleanses it, makes it fit to be the body of his eternal Son. It must be a body just like ours if the true miracle of Christmas is to take place: the miracle that our bodies, yours and mine with all their imperfections and sins, can finally be offered, perfected, to God our creator.

We can never look at the Christmas story without bearing in mind its point, which is the salvation of the world – notice that word again: God acts to save this world, the world which he created and loves, the world which without his Son's incarnation cannot return to be what he created it to be. Why was he made incarnate by the Holy Spirit and the Virgin Mary? The creed gives its reasons: in the traditional translation, 'for us men and our salvation'. And our passage from Hebrews shows that this is the very point. As we have seen, it begins with the

---

1 That is why I believe those theologians are wrong, absolutely wrong, who developed the doctrine of Mary's immaculate conception. CEG.

psalmist's claim that God does not want mere empty sacrifices. But he does want a sacrifice of one kind, and one kind alone: he wants the free and joyful gift of proper, loving, human lives. And so our passage ends, 'we have been made holy through the sacrifice of the body of Jesus Christ once for all'. Our theme of the body, the worldly, material body, returns.

Through the power of his Spirit, this child, though never free from the backwards tug of the fallen flesh he bears, is called to make an offering of a perfect human life to his Father. In his previous chapter, Hebrews has made just this point, speaking of Jesus who 'through the eternal Spirit offered himself unblemished to God' (9.14). The fact that he is born of a woman, an ordinary woman, reminds us that there is nothing automatic about this process. He has to bear the burden of our wicked past while himself doing no wrong. And he does so in order that we, like him, can, by his sacrifice and the Holy Spirit's energies, be at the last brought perfect before God's throne of grace.

III

'Sacrifice and offering you did not desire, but a body you prepared for me.' The greatest miracle of all is not the virgin birth, but that the Son of God goes through all of this for us. He became poor so that we might become rich; he was for us made to be sin who knew no sin; he empties himself so that we might be full. Scripture piles on the images to attempt to bring out the breathtaking love and self-giving that this involves.

'Sacrifice and offering you did not desire, but a body you prepared for me.' Here we have the denial of the need for sacrifice for the sake of the sacrifice that matters, the self-giving that is to be the mark of this man's life and death from now on. We saw at the beginning of this sermon, it is the worship of the creation not the creator that is the root of our troubles. And so God himself goes to the root: to the body and its troubled and corrupt heart, in order to enable it to make the kind of sacrifice that God truly requires of us. The psalmists knew this already: 'the sacrifices of God are a broken spirit; a broken and contrite heart' – and notice that word again – 'you will not despise'. It is this that Christina Rossetti takes up in that hymn – top of the Classic FM chart at present – 'In the bleak midwinter'.[2] 'What can I give him, poor as I am?' – and we are indeed poor in all the important senses – 'give him my heart'. His sacrifice of his body – his whole life – enables us to give something of ours, as Paul tells his Roman correspondents: 'offer your bodies as a living sacrifice, holy and pleasing to God'. Once again, we are returned to the theme of life in this world.

Of course, in our own strength and as we are, we are unable to do what is required of us. We are unlike Jesus, in that the backward tug to the old world remains too strong for us so long as we remain in our mortal bodies. Yet, and this is the absolute miracle of this event, he makes us holy, makes us acceptable to God. God accepts us through him. And there is more than that. The Spirit who renewed in this case the tired and corrupt flesh from which Jesus' body was formed is available to us also: that is the point of the whole affair. We don't even have to ask for his presence, though we should and must.

And what do we ask? For the renewing and warming of our hearts. In *A Christmas Carol* Dickens got it quite right. Scrooge's worship of money could only be wiped out by something stronger. There is something of Scrooge in all of us, that fearfulness that makes us seek security in this world alone. Yet our calling is not to renounce this world but to live in it as God's creation. This does not rule out sharing the festivities of Christmas; indeed, it liberates us to share them properly, as the free children of the good creator. And so to end by repeating the very opening words of the service: 'Many, O Lord my God, are the wonders you have done. The things you planned for us, no-one can recount them to you. Were I to speak and tell of them, they would be too many to declare'.

---

2 *Rejoice and Sing*, 162.

7

Materialism

> Therefore, my friends, I implore you by God's mercy to offer your very selves to him: a living sacrifice, dedicated and fit for his acceptance, the worship of mind and heart.
>
> (Rom. 12:1)

3 OCTOBER 1999

Readings: Lev. 9.1–8; Rom. 12.1–16; Lk. 7.29–35

I

One of the conferences I was at recently was prefaced by a service, at which we were presented with a fifty-minute sermon, forty minutes of which were devoted to telling us about the nature of the 'postmodern' world in which we live. The preacher regaled us with an account of how we have all become, or are in danger of becoming, rootless and unconnected individuals, with no shared values or belief in truth. Perhaps most telling was the graffito he had seen around Cambridge: 'George Washington could not tell a lie; Richard Nixon could not tell the truth; Clinton does not know the difference'. This was an exaggerated account of the modern world, but not entirely without truth, as two articles in a recent newspaper suggested. The first was by a journalist who claimed that the world today was so boring that all he could do to make it tolerable was to shop, the result of which was that he had all kinds of clothes that he does not need. The second was more serious, and quoted a report that says that one of the reasons for the widespread breakdown of marriages is that people are now simply more selfish, unwilling to give up their desires and activities in the interest of stable relationships.

We all know that there is much in this. Many forces operating in the modern world are seeking to turn us all into units with no concern with or interest in anything but ourselves. But this means that we are living in a fool's paradise. Some teachers the other evening were saying that children have to carry round with them all day every bit of clothing, books and equipment they need at school, they can't leave things in cloakrooms or desks, because they would simply be stolen. We live in a world where trust is in danger of disappearing. The point is a simple one: the quest for self-satisfaction, for self-realization at the cost of others, does little else than increase the sum of human misery, including that of the one who seeks it. Our plight – and we are all bound up in this, even though we may not share the extremes – is that we seek our own good, often at the expense of our neighbour's, when we know that it is both wrong and self-destructive. Our world, especially its commercial interests, is in many ways forcing upon us a way of being that wrenches us away from our true selves, our true being.

II

And now for something, apparently, completely different. Let me begin with a brief look at the text, then I shall move to the Old Testament reading, and then back to our text again. 'Therefore, my friends, I implore you by God's mercy to offer your very selves to him: a living sacrifice, dedicated and fit for his acceptance, the worship of mind and heart.' It is that word 'sacrifice' I want to concentrate on. As the commentary I read pointed out, this verse is full of sacrificial language: 'offer', 'holy', 'well-pleasing' are all technical terms from that strange religious world we call the world of sacrifice. And it is strange for us, or so it seems. Does the worship of God really require this? Well, for the Old Testament it did, but for neither (most) Jews nor Christians does it now. Leviticus has many apparently strange instructions for the organization of sacrifices, and we may think they have little to say to us. Yet I think that would

Materialism

be wrong. I have a student studying the subject, and he would tell you that when you hand over a five-pound note in a shop, you are doing exactly the same as the ancient Israelite in the temple.

Let me try to explain something of the meaning of this. When you give or spend money, you are giving something of yourself. Money is a medium of exchange, as we say: we exchange the fruits of our labour for food or clothes or entertainment. If you are going to understand sacrifice, you have to see that sacrifice is also a medium of exchange, in a very similar way. In handing over money, we exchange part of ourselves, of who and what we are, for something else. That, I think, is why we find giving money away so difficult, and why the man who has nothing to do but shop for himself is so depressing. He is giving a bit of himself for something he does not need or really want. And the point of the Leviticus passage is this. When people give something to God, in this case an animal – the creatures by which people nourish and clothe themselves – they are giving something of themselves, to come near to God cleansed and made holy.

After the death of Jesus, things change. That is because he is now the temple, he is the place where people meet with their God. And that takes us back to the New Testament text. Let me repeat it. 'Therefore, my friends, I implore you by God's mercy to offer your very selves to him: a living sacrifice, dedicated and fit for his acceptance, the worship of mind and heart.' This is Romans 12, and for eleven chapters Paul has expatiated on the goodness of God, Christ's self-giving *sacrificial* death on the cross, and all it means. Those eleven chapters are summed up in our verse by the expression, 'By the mercies of God'. In Christ, God has given us himself, Jesus has become the medium of exchange – we might say the coinage in which our relations with our creator are now centred. 'You know the grace of our Lord Jesus Christ, who, though he was rich, for your sakes became poor, so that you through his poverty might become rich' (2 Cor. 8.9).

And, Paul is saying, there is only one response to be made to such sheer generosity: gratitude. Far from spending his money on himself, we might say, God gives his Son, he cuts off his own right arm, so that we in turn might be freed from the self-centredness that blights our lives and those of others. So Paul says: 'Give your selves' – in a literal translation, 'give your bodies – as a living sacrifice, holy and acceptable to God'. There are two things – well, at least, but I'll stick at that – to be said about this. First, notice that the sacrifice is *living*. This isn't a denial of life, it is life in all its fullness; quite the opposite of days dedicated to the god of the shopping mall, that cathedral of modern-day living. 'The glory of God is a human being truly alive' – that wonderful saying from Irenaeus makes the point. It is said that when the nineteenth-century divine, E. B. Pusey, was converted, he resolved never to smile again. That is not, in my view, the point. This sacrifice is meant to be alive: given to God in sheer thankfulness for his goodness and mercy, his self-giving in his Son Jesus.

The second point is this. Notice very carefully the words: 'give your bodies as a living sacrifice', in the singular. This is spoken to a church, and it says: at the heart is the thing that you do together. Of course we offer our lives to God in thanksgiving individually, but only as the result of all that we do together – our worship, especially, but also our learning, our social occasions and our business meetings, even our disagreements. The heart of the sacrifice is our response as a church, through what happens with this group of God's people meeting here, and only through that are our individual responses made to God. To return to the monetary theme: the coinage in which we repay God is the thankfulness as a result of which we praise his name in worship week by week and praise it in lives offered to him, rather than to the gods of the marketplace.

III

The point of the word 'bodies' in this verse is that our offering, our sacrifice of praise, is not just of spiritual, religious things, but of our whole lives: that is to say, our eating and drinking, our spending, our relations with spouses, children, friends and all the others with whom we have to do and, perhaps especially, our daily work. That is not an invitation to be self-absorbed, anxious about everything we do, over-scrupulous about enjoying ourselves. Life is to be lived. The point is that it is to be lived to and with other people, not in the spirit of that journalist who had nothing better to do to assuage his boredom. We are not in the business of making people feel guilty all the time, but of freeing them to offer what they do to God out of sheer gratitude. We have been loved, and God will enable us – sometimes, of course, not always – to love in return.

I remember in my time hearing a number of sermons which have referred to the hymn containing the verse,

> Take my silver and my gold,
> Not a mite would I withhold[1]

The congregation is challenged – sometimes when funds are low! – to ask whether they can really sing it and mean it. It is thus used to apply pressure, to increase guilt. Can we really sing it honestly? In one sense, of course not. But the important point is that we call on our Lord to shape our attitudes to money and all the other good things of life. Can we offer to the glory of God the money we spend on this and that, the music we make and listen to, the visits to the theatre or cinema? We have to think about that but not be dominated by scrupulousness. Calvin somewhere says that if people start worrying about whether it is or is not right to wear silk, they

---

1 *Rejoice and Sing*, 371.

will end up worrying if they wear sackcloth. The Christian life is a serious thing, but not like that. It is here above all that we need to recall the words of our text: it is not grit the teeth, increase the guilt but, 'By the mercies of God'. There is only one reason for doing what we do, and that is sheer gratitude.

Of course, that does not always come easy. Sometimes we do have to grit our teeth and address ourselves to things we do not want to do. But that is only a holding operation, a second best when all else fails. Sometimes we don't see the point of it and want to run away, to escape into the safety of our heads or our homes. That is only to be expected of those who are treading a difficult and serious path. But what counts is where we look when we are in these moods, not at our worries, failures and selfishness, but to the one who has already borne their cost: Jesus, who has been there before us, 'who, for the joy that was set before him, endured the cross, despising the shame, and is set at the right hand of the throne of God'.

8

Heaven and the Saints

> On the gates were written the names of the twelve tribes of Israel. . . . The wall of the city had twelve foundations, and on them were the names of the twelve apostles of the lamb.
> (Rev. 21.12, 14)

ALL SAINTS, 1 NOVEMBER 1998

Readings: 1 Kgs 19.9b–11; Rev. 21.1–14; Mt. 13.24–30, 37–43

I

It is one of the unfortunate episodes in the history of the church that for a long period preachers and others assured their listeners that the punishment of sinners in hell redounded to the glory of God; that not only God, but the saved were expected to rejoice in the suffering of the wicked. Is God glorified in the punishment of a sinner? Is it not expressly said in Scripture that God is a God who desires the repentance, not the death, of a sinner? Can he then glory in their punishment? If not, however, what is the place of those descriptions of the punishment of the wicked, for example in our two readings – of the wheat and the tares, and the 'second death'?

Then there is a second problem. In art and literature, much has been made of the pains of hell: details expounded in often almost pathological detail in order to show the sheer awfulness of the pains the damned will suffer. That is mistaken for two reasons. First, it is frightening people into belief, rather than offering them good news of free salvation. For Jesus, things go the other way round: the kingdom of God is imminent – repent. We do indeed need to repent, not from fear of hell, but because the Gospel sets us free to do so. The good news of the kingdom comes first, inviting us in. And the second reason is that such an overemphasis on hell is, again, false to Scripture. The Bible does use images of fire but does not go into detail. Fire is that which consumes, burns up rubbish. It is an image, not meant to be a literal description of hell and certainly not an encouragement to expand on the pain. In the parable we heard from Matthew, the farmer's rubbish heap is an image for the storing of the food and the burning of weeds, not for composting the weeds eternally and painfully. Similarly, in our reading from Revelation: the 'fiery lake of burning sulphur' is explained as the second death, the death from which there is no waking up, and does not refer to punishment going on for ever.

We must not exaggerate that side of things, as has often been done, but that does not mean that we should not take the images seriously. Something is at stake in the images of the wheat and the weeds, the saints and the wicked. Today is All Saints' Day, and it reminds us that there is a group of people called saints, and also implies that there is another group who are not. All are indeed invited into God's kingdom, but there are kinds of acts which, if engaged in persistently, exclude us from it. At the heart of the Gospel there is free forgiveness of sins. But what if that gift is rejected in such a way that we deliberately throw it back in the face of the giver, continuing to behave as if we do not belong to God? Just as offence against the law of the land may exclude you from civil society – by being sent to prison, for example – so by certain forms of behaviour, we may exclude ourselves from the presence of God. In the New Testament there are varying, but generally similar, lists of such behaviour and they include both public and private acts – those, we might say, committed by both President Clinton and General Pinochet, to use a couple of examples to hand. The lists are often based on the Ten Commandments, whose deep seriousness they reflect, because they crystallize what is expected of us in our relations with God and our neighbour. In the reading from Revelation there is one such list: 'the cowardly, the unbelieving, the vile, the murderers, the sexually immoral, those who practise magic arts, the idolaters and liars'. Of course, we are all at least some of those things some of the time. The point is that persisting in them, unrepentantly hardening our hearts against God and our neighbour, excludes us from the company of the godly. Those who deliberately refuse, place themselves in danger of final rejection. Living before God and in the world is a serious matter, like marriage, not to be undertaken lightly. One of the things about being among the saints is that we confess, as honestly as we can, and week by week, our failure to remain true to our calling, and to ask God's grace in enabling us to live godly lives. And that leads me into the main part of the sermon. Who are those saints whose day it is?

II

A simple answer would be those who do not take the matter of living the Gospel lightly. But to get to the heart of the matter, we must look more closely at some of the things said in our text. Towards the end of his vision, in chapter 21 as we have heard, the seer of Patmos sees 'a new heaven and a new earth', and that sets the tone for all that he is to say. There has been, in Christ, a great act of redemption, of cleansing, of renewal – so much so that even the sea, the waters of chaos that would inundate the good creation is no more – and we know what that means these days. Then come the great promises: the New Jerusalem comes down out of heaven, 'like a bride adorned for her husband'. And the words are heard, 'Now the dwelling of God is with men . . . They will be his people . . . and he will wipe away every tear from their eyes. There will be no more death or mourning or crying or pain, for the old order of things has passed away'.

That is the order of the promise: because of what God has done in Christ, the present is lived in hope of the final renewal of all things, of the new heaven and new earth which will take the place of the tired old order. This general affirmation of the newness of all things is followed by promises to particular people. 'I am the Alpha and the Omega, the Beginning and the End. To him who is thirsty I will give to drink without cost from the spring of the water of life.' There is the offer: life without cost, good measure, pressed down and brimming over, the free and overwhelming love of him who died on the cross for the children of men. Unlike the free gifts on offer in the modern marketplace, this comes absolutely without strings. It is simply the outcome of God's overwhelming generosity for his people. To be sure, to be of any use it has to be taken up, but that does not make it any the less generous and free. 'He who overcomes will inherit all this, and I will be his God.' This book sees human life as a battle, a battle fought indeed in the aftermath of that battle won for us on the cross, but a battle none the less, a battle against evil within and without, against what Hebrews calls the sin that clings so closely. It is here that appears the list of vices to which I have already referred and which exclude the wicked from the kingdom. Accepting the free gift involves a life of moral seriousness. And that enables me to add to the definition of the saints among whom we are: the saints are simply those who accept that victory which is won for them on the cross and set out to realize it in overcoming those features of their lives which do continue to hold them back from full life in the kingdom.

So far, then, we have three things: the vision of the world renewed; the promises to those who accept the gift; the seriousness with which we take up the life of the people of God. But then there is a fourth thing, which provides a fuller account of the plan of the heavenly city. The angel offers John a tour of the heavenly city. Just two details are needed to make the point. The city has twelve gates, and on them are written the names of the twelve tribes of Israel. And it has twelve foundation stones, and 'on them were the names of the twelve apostles of the lamb'. And there – continuing the picture of the city – is the final building block of our definition of the saints. They are simply those who live in the tradition of the people of Israel and who hear and believe the words of the apostles. The point of all this is that we are not on our own. We are not individual strivers after moral improvement, but those who live together in the city of God, the city of Abraham and his descendants, of all who have accepted the gift of salvation in Jesus Christ. That is who the saints are.

III

At least three of the people who have preached regularly from this pulpit in living memory learned something about the leading of worship sitting in the chapel of Mansfield College, Oxford. That is sometimes described as the most catholic building in Oxford because of the remarkable stained-glass windows, which contain portraits of well-known Christians from every age, right up until the building of the chapel last century. In recent decades, I have attended two funerals of teachers whose example marks every sermon I preach here, and if the chapel were to be built today, there is little doubt that they would be among the stained-glass portraits. Many of those appearing in the windows were not saints in the narrower sense of the term: indeed, they sometimes defended their vision of the faith with a ruthlessness quite unbecoming a follower of the crucified Lord. Similar things will be said of us, but that is not the point. The first lesson to be learned is that the saints are many and various, with different strengths and weaknesses, but nonetheless saints.

I remember John Marsh, one of those whose funerals I have attended, confessing that as he got older he didn't get any better, still felt himself dogged by foibles and weaknesses that held him back. Perhaps he was wrong. The point is, however, that he faithfully travelled the way of Jesus Christ, living only in the light of forgiveness and promise. That, simply, is what it is to be one of the saints, to whose greater company he has now gone.

And the second lesson is this. I remember a sermon that took us around those stained-glass saints, in the light of the text that we are surrounded by a cloud of witnesses. And the preacher said: we think that text refers to a lot of people looking at us. But that mistakes what they are witnessing to: not us, but Jesus. To be one of the saints is to be among those who in every age, from Abraham until now, witness to Jesus Christ our Lord, in whom rest all the promises of God and, particularly, the promise that we, too, will be named among those who overcome and will inherit the promises of our Lord.

9
Christianity and Islam

After his birth, astrologers from the east arrived in Jerusalem.
(Mt. 2.1b)

FESTIVAL OF EPIPHANY, 6 JANUARY 2002

Readings: Mt. 2.1–12; Isa. 60.1–6; Eph. 3.1–12

I

'After his birth, astrologers from the east arrived in Jerusalem.' On 11 September last, birds of a rather different feather arrived in New York, also from the East. As one journalist commented, 'we are being made frighteningly aware of the implacable ferocity of the East', a ferocity of which Scripture, too, knows – as witness the story of the slaughter of the innocents by King Herod. We tend to become mystical about the East, the place of ancient wisdom, with 1960s hippies and modern Buddhists alike seeking enlightenment. It is surprising how often the East is mentioned in the early chapters of Genesis: east of Eden, Abraham travelling east, and so on. These men come from the east, bringing strange gifts and leaving trouble in their wake. They appear in many a nativity play and are part of our Christmas. Specifically, they belong at Epiphany, which for once arrives actually on a Sunday. Because they are the first foreigners to acknowledge Jesus, they have traditionally provided a way into his universal claims, his claim on the allegiance of every man, woman and child on earth, the divine king of all creation (Isa. 60, Eph. 3). The creed puts it thus,'Light from light, true God from true God', and similarly, first thing Christmas morning we sang, 'True God of true God, light of light eternal, lo! thou abhorrest not the virgin's womb'. Let us explore something of those universal claims, in part against the dark backcloth of the rather different claim for universal allegiance expressed in New York.

II

In a recent article, Neil MacGregor illustrated from the history of art how the Magi had experienced a progressive inflation from their simple biblical beginnings. In Matthew, they are simply astrologers, and not numbered or named. Let us pause to look at Scripture before examining the fate of the Magi. This is perhaps the only place in the Bible where astrologers are given a single good word. In the very first chapter of Genesis, it is made clear that the stars do not rule the fates of men. 'He made the stars also': in a single dismissive phrase the writer reduces them to lights in the sky, placed in their courses at the sovereign creator's command. That we have entered a new age of superstition was indicated by the fact that even one of the broadsheet newspapers last week filled half of one of its seasonal pages with the writings of an astrologer. In a fable in Daniel, Nebuchadnezzar threatened to put all his astrologers to death for failing to tell him what he had dreamed and what it meant, while Daniel saves the day by listening to his God. Similarly the second Isaiah (47.12ff) scorns the astrologers and soothsayers of the Babylonian state, which will be reduced to ruins. His prophecy comes straight from God, not via the stars.

What, then, are these dubious characters doing in the Gospels? Some early writers suggest that they are laying down their magic arts before the true king, abandoning their astrology now that the true king is here. The majority view is that they are simply paying homage to Jesus, the ancient wisdom acknowledging the infant Messiah. Whatever be the truth of that, it is clear that Matthew is introducing a universal note in his Gospel, that the grace of God reaches even these disreputable men, who proceed to mess things up by blabbing to Herod and getting children killed. As a recent commentator points out, both here and elsewhere Matthew introduces a note of scandal into the Gospel story. In his genealogy of Jesus' ancestors in the previous chapter, not only are women included, but among them are far from respectable ones. Similarly, later in the Gospel it is the prostitutes and tax collectors who are the objects of Jesus' particular attention. The Gospel is for everyone, even – especially – those who are despised and irreligious.

The universal thrust of the gospel was emphasized in a different way by the development of the tradition of the wise men or even kings. The Venerable Bede even found them names – 'names of wondrous resonance – Caspar, Melchior and Balthasar'[1] – and their supposed burial place was identified. MacGregor uses the National Gallery's *The Adoration of the Kings*, 1500–15 by Jan Gossaert to show that these shadowy figures were used in the service of debate about the oneness of all mankind before God. In this and other paintings we find an old man, a middle-aged man and a younger man; there are representatives of the three known continents – Europe, Africa and Asia. There is no woman – though the prominence of Mary makes up for that. One prominent feature is that they are all rich – 'by far the most expensively dressed kings in Trafalgar Square'. What is lost is the scandal of Matthew's account. The Magi have become respectable kings, indeed used to teach a lesson about the right use of power and wealth in Christian society, but respectable nonetheless. The story is far more murky than this, as the slaughter of the innocents continues to remind us. Yet there is something in the painting which is absolutely right: the utter nakedness of the new-born child. 'This king has no clothes. The pale body, which will again be naked and again the centre of attention at the Crucifixion, tells only of poverty and vulnerability.' That, as we shall see, is the key to it all.

---

1 Neil MacGregor, 'A Picture of all Humanity', *The Spectator*, 15–22 December 2001, p. 69.

III

'After his birth, astrologers from the east arrived in Jerusalem.' They may have been from further east, but we must remember that Christianity is essentially an Eastern religion, formed in that general region that has given the world more than one of its great faiths. 'Salvation is of the Jews', and the Jews are an Eastern, Semitic people, as indeed are the Arabs. Nor is it only a matter of the origins of our faith; it has to do with its present reality also. It might appear that although our faith was born in the East, it has become essentially a Western religion, as it is often charged with being. Certainly, that is where much of it has been shaped, and yet it is far from being restricted to the West today. Indeed, in the West it is in relative decline, while in places like China and Africa it has grown explosively. What began in a small near-eastern land has now become a universal faith, making claims to be true everywhere and for everyone.

And that is the problem, for in that respect Islam is the same, although in that respect only. However distorted may be their vision of Islam, Mr Bin Laden and his fellows are true to their faith in seeing that it, too, makes universal claims. And here, if we are to begin to understand what is going on in our world, we must appreciate that although politically the current crisis represents the challenge of an Eastern group to a great Western power, the religious undercurrents contain also a clash of religious views. We can understand it by making some comparisons. A first is that although both Christianity and Islam have fundamentalist forms, Christian fundamentalists do not believe in bombing and killing their way to dominion.[2] A second difference is to be found in something recently observed by an American journalist, that although many Christians have in the past few months gone out of their way to say nice things about Islam, the compliment is never returned. However we may

---

2 It is important to acknowledge in this context, however, that Christians have in the past tried to impose their beliefs, culture and political authority by force.

think it right to deal with it, we have to come to terms with the fact that for most Muslims, a state that is not Islamic is not truly a state. Islam makes an absolute political claim on its adherents which we, with our tradition of the separation of church and state, will do well to understand. It is a claim for absolute allegiance which is fundamentally different in form from that which Jesus makes, however badly we his followers succeed in realizing it.

Christianity is like Islam in making universal claims of every human being. 'Light from light, true God from true God' is the claim that our creed makes of Jesus, the child in the manger and the executed criminal on the cross. He is the universal Lord of creation become man for us. But the fact that it is as a naked baby that he makes his epiphany is precisely the point. You cannot be forced to confess a baby as the universal God, though sad to say attempts have sometimes been made. One of the things for which our dissenting ancestors died is that Christian faith demands free response. The cross is a demonstration of the way God inculcates belief, not at the point of a sword, but by the Spirit's convincing us that this is the power and the wisdom of God made man and crucified for us.

Such a faith requires, as we are taught, that we should pray for those who despitefully use us, accepting that following in the way of him who was crucified may mean suffering for our confession. That has always been the right way: not seeking martyrdom – and certainly not martyrdom by murderous suicide – but accepting it if necessary. That is not to make any judgement about the different and difficult question of whether our government has the right and the duty to defend us by war against regimes that harbour terrorists. As a matter of fact, I think that it has, though I also think that it would be wrong to do it in the name of our faith. That need not divide us as Christians, for our gospel makes one thing clear: that ours is a universal faith, but one whose claims are demonstrated in one way and one way alone:

> Truth of our life, Mary's child,
> you tell us that God is good;
> prove it is true, Mary's child,
> go to your cross of wood.[3]

The one who is 'Light from light, true God from true God' comes to our world to be born naked and to die similarly on a cross. That God raised him from the dead is demonstration of the fact that God is not only good but also sovereign – the sovereign Lord who rules the stars in their courses – and that we can leave the outcome of our troubled human history to him.

---

3 *Rejoice and Sing*, 188.

10

The Problem of Evil

> I am the Lord and there is no other. I form light and create darkness, I bring prosperity and create disaster; I, the Lord, do all these things.
>
> (Isa. 45.6, 7)

23 SEPTEMBER 2001

Readings: Isa. 45.1–8; 2 Thess. 2.1–12; Lk. 13.1–9

I

Many of our traditional prayers begin with the words, 'Almighty God'. There is much in our theology about the power of God. God, we say, is omnipotent: he is all-powerful, can do anything he likes, and all the rest. And, indeed, it is found in our creed: 'I believe in God the Father Almighty'. Not surprisingly, lots of people have problems with this, and two in particular. The first is this. It is easy to depict God as a heavenly tyrant, one who by sheer power forces things into his mould, and against this there has arisen in recent centuries a movement known as protest atheism. If God is like that, then we will reject him, say a number of moderns, who regard God as the enemy to be opposed. The second problem is in some ways similar, though in others the opposite. If God is so powerful, why does he not see to it that his world is run somewhat more benevolently? Why, to use a common way of putting it, does he allow crazed terrorists to fly aircraft into buildings, to kill indiscriminately? Could he not intervene to stop it, if he is really all-powerful? There is a famous depiction of the challenge in a novel by that great Christian novelist, Dostoevsky. If God allows the suffering of one innocent child, is that not enough to reject him – simply to return the ticket, as a character in the novel claims?

The terrible events in New York, whose long-term outcome is still so unpredictable, sum up all the problems we have with the idea that God is omnipotent. Sometimes the world seems too uncertain, too wicked, too overwhelmingly hostile to appear the work of a good and all-powerful God. The problem becomes worse when it seems that perhaps the perpetrators of the ill claim to be obeying God's will in what they call a holy war. What, then, shall we make of it all? We can, if we like, appeal to human freedom. Are we not free to do evil if we decide? Why blame God? That, however, simply pushes the problem a stage back. Who creates these beings with this overwhelming capacity for evil? In one brief sermon, we cannot solve all the problems, and, indeed, that is not what sermons are for. What I shall try to do is to concentrate on one problem. The creed calls God 'almighty', and in doing so it is being true to Scripture. What does it mean, however? Let us examine something of the light the Scriptures have to throw on our topic.

II

The writer we call the Second Isaiah ministered to the people of Israel in their exile in Babylon. Carried away from their home, they began to wonder if God was still bothered with them. Isaiah's message is straightforward. They should not suppose that because they are away from their land they are outside God's care. The God of these chapters – 40–55 of the book of Isaiah – is the universal creator, who rules heaven and earth, and everything that happens within his creation. Nor is he restricted in what he can do to calling only on those who believe in him. Even kings who refuse to acknowledge him bring about his purposes despite themselves. Thus, in an astonishing passage, the prophet calls Cyrus, the King of Persia, his anointed; the servant who will bring about his purposes of destroying the power of Babylon: 'Cyrus, whose right hand I

The Problem of Evil

take hold of to subdue nations before him'; 'though you do not acknowledge me . . . though you have not acknowledged me' (vv. 4, 5). And he does it for the sake of his people Israel, so that they may return to the land from which they had been taken: 'for the sake of Jacob my servant, of Israel my chosen'.

But the purposes of God stretch beyond Israel, who is his servant for a purpose: 'so that from the rising of the sun to its setting men may know that there is none besides me'. And he continues in words that provide the text for today: 'I am the Lord and there is no other. I form light and create darkness, I bring prosperity and create disaster; I, the Lord, do all these things'. 'I bring prosperity and I create disaster.' That is the difficult thing for us to encompass. Does God actually bring about evil? Well, Isaiah is not the only one to suggest so, and Amos 3.6 is similar in its thrust. 'When disaster comes to a city, has not the Lord caused it?' We have to accept the full implications of what is being said here. Nothing, even the worst thing that happens, is outside the Lord's control, at least in the sense that he permits it to happen. That does not mean, of course, either that the Americans deserved what happened to them or that the same can be said of what they deal out in their turn. Things are much more complicated than that. Remember what Jesus said about a similar, if smaller disaster: 'Or those eighteen who died when the tower in Siloam fell on them – do you think they were more guilty than all the others living in Jerusalem?' (Lk. 13.4). What God is doing and why is rarely clear to us at the time – except that we know that things are not outside his ordering.

There are three things about the way things work that we must learn from all this:

1

God works long term, allowing things to take their course. Rome was not built in a day; a child does not become an adult overnight; and so it is with everything in God's creation. One of the points made in Genesis 1, with its creation over a period of 'days', is that God makes a world which only becomes what it is over time. In this case, we are looking at something additional, as well. Once evil has taken hold, things take even longer. God allows things to take their course, not because he cannot do anything else, but because that is the nature of created things. They neither become what they are instantly, nor are they healed of their sickness overnight. There is no instant salvation, no magical removal of evil at a stroke, at least until time has run its full course.

2

Yet, if we are to believe the Bible, evil is never allowed to run out of control. It is indeed true that evil can become entrenched in whole nations, as we saw happened in Germany during the last century, so that even innocent people seem to be caught up into doing things quite against their true selves. It seems to be the case that this rogue form of Islam has a similar way of creating fanaticism and moral blindness, killing almost for the sake of it. But the way of all these systems is doomed. The reading we heard from 2 Thessalonians makes a similar point. Paul speaks of someone 'who sets himself up in God's temple, proclaiming himself to be God'; he will do appalling damage, but there is one who holds the evil one back, 'till he is taken out of the way'. Notice too the way the story of the coming of evil into God's good world is told in Genesis. At each stage, it brings disaster in its train, yet at each stage, God in his mercy sees to it that its toll is restricted. My favourite example is Cain, who is punished for the murder of his brother and yet is given a mark so that no one will punish him further. So we must believe of these events we fear so much that they may indeed be fearful, but in the mercy of God they will be restricted within limits, so that some good may eventually result.

3

And that takes us to the third point, which is perhaps the most important of all. Where does God reveal his power and his

The Problem of Evil

mercy, his limiting and defeat of evil? And the answer is, on the cross of Jesus, the power and the wisdom and the mercy of God in action. There evil, the greatest evil that would destroy goodness and love, is faced and overcome, and its doom ensured. This is the basis of our confidence both that God allows things to take their time and yet shows that from within our time and space he takes charge of them in an omnipotent way – omnipotent, for evil has no answer to the one who conquers it by love alone, refusing to use the weapons of the enemy. In that we must trust. It does not necessarily mean, I believe, that we can never support the use of force, even war, to overcome the threats to our world. It certainly means that we usually cannot support the use of force in coming to terms with those in our daily life who do us harm, for revenge is ruled out for the Christian. But proper punishment is not revenge, and nor is the forcible restraint of the violent. When the last war, the war against the evil of Nazism, broke out, my father was a pacifist. By the end of the war, he had decided that he was wrong. There are no easy answers to these things; whatever we do, however, we must do them in the light of, and trusting in the power of, the victory of the cross.

III

What are we to make of our creed in the light of all this? Notice the way in which the creed actually speaks. First of all, it speaks of 'God the Father Almighty'. The almighty God, the omnipotent, the one who is Lord of all things – 'I am the Lord and there is no other' – is not simply an omnipotent deity – and certainly not the tyrant whose ticket we must return – but the one who is the Lord and Father of our Lord Jesus Christ. On my sixtieth birthday, some of my students gave me an icon of Jesus,[1] the pantocrator, a representation of the risen and ascended Lord in glory. It is a representation of a heavenly

---

[1] Also mentioned in the sermon preached on 4 February 2001.

monarch and ruler, awesome in his power, but he remains the crucified. His power is the greatest possible power we can imagine, because it achieves its end through the merciful means of the cross. He lets evil take its course, but only to a degree. His answer to evil is good, to hatred love. In sum, we are speaking of the power that takes shape in the love that died even for those who sought to put it to death. That is real, omnipotent power but, as we have seen, it does not achieve its ends overnight. It is firm, relentless and will not let go until evil is driven from the earth and tears are wiped from all eyes. In the meantime, we the people of God can but live by the faith that this is indeed the case and the hope that comes from the resurrection.

Second, the creed associates that power with creation: 'the Father Almighty, maker of heaven and earth'. This takes us right back to our text, with the words of the Second Isaiah. 'I am the Lord and there is no other. I form light and create darkness, I bring prosperity and create disaster; I, the Lord, do all these things.' The crucified Jesus wields the power of the Lord of all creation.

What then is to be our attitude to the events of recent weeks and those unknown consequences we still can but fear? Our response is first to pray that God will use this evil event in the long term to bring about good. Already there have been some good responses: Israel and the Palestinians appear to have at least been made to think a bit more carefully, for example.[2] And our second response must come in the light of what we believe about the cross and resurrection. The key to it, as we have already seen, is the long term. John Maynard Keynes famously replied to a comment like this that in the long term we are all dead, but dead in the hope of the resurrection of the dead. In that light, listen to the daily news bulletins as the events unfold.

---

2 It should be noted that this example was given in 2001 and not 2006.

11

Prophecy and Proof

> So was fulfilled what was said through the prophets.
>
> (Mt. 2.23)

SUNDAY BEFORE EPIPHANY, 5 JANUARY 2003

Readings: Isa. 49.1–7; Eph. 3.1–12; Matt. 2.13–23

I

It is a mistake to try too hard to prove something – like the lady one can protest too much. It was once joked that it was only when theologians began to produce proofs of God's existence that people began to doubt it. Indeed, part of our modern-day difficulty in getting people to take the faith seriously comes from the way efforts were made some centuries ago to defend the gospel against attacks. It is a long story, but in the eighteenth century in particular defenders of the faith made appeal to two things: that Jesus fulfilled Old Testament prophecy, and that he performed miracles. It is the former, the fulfilment of prophecy, about which I want to speak today, the Sunday before Epiphany. At this season, we concern ourselves with the manifestation of Jesus not only to his own people but also to the Gentiles represented by the three astrologers. How are we best to commend the gospel to the sceptical world of which we are a part, in which astrology is often taken more seriously than the prophecies of Scripture?

Let me return to the question of the fulfilment of prophecy. The appeal to it in the eighteenth century met the fate of most of those who protest too much. It soon enough came to be argued that it is not obvious that Jesus does fulfil prophecy.

Isaiah's 'wonderful counsellor', for example, was claimed not to be about Jesus at all, but about a contemporary event, and so one could go on with many other examples. Some critical scholars have similarly attempted to take apart Matthew's use of Scripture. We heard for our gospel reading the second part of Matthew 2, the series of events that took place after the departure back home of the Magi. The story is of the flight into Egypt, the slaughter of the innocents, and the eventual return of the holy family to Israel after the death of Herod. In this passage, there are three appeals to the fulfilment of Scripture, to our modern eyes perhaps rather wooden and unconvincing, and critics have been eager to point out that in their original setting they have nothing to do with Jesus. Let us look at them.

II

The first concerns the flight of Joseph and Mary into Egypt, to save the child from murder by Herod – a subject popular with painters of biblical scenes. Egypt lies deep in Israel's history as the place of asylum for Jacob and his family – and later of slavery for Israel. It marks the birthplace of Israel as a nation. After recording that the family remained there until the death of Herod, Matthew explains the point of the journey by a citation from the prophet Hosea: 'out of Egypt I called my son'. Jesus is lined up with Israel, indeed with the very history of her foundation. In the chapter from which Matthew quotes, Hosea is chiding Israel for her disobedience. Here, the Gospel suggests, is an obedient Son, called out of Egypt for God's saving purposes – the true Israelite. And the need of that salvation is expressed in the second episode, telling of the slaughter of the children of Bethlehem. This time Matthew takes a comment from Jeremiah (31.15): 'A voice is heard in Ramah . . . Rachel weeping for her children'. In its original setting, the prophecy is a promise of comfort: Rachel may be weeping, but there is hope of a restoration. Is that Matthew's purpose also? We can't

Prophecy and Proof

tell, except that he wants us to know that some such disaster had been predicted: that prophecy helps us to understand the meaning of this terrible event. That reference is strange enough, but the third is stranger. On returning to Israel, Joseph is warned that Judaea is not much safer than it was under Herod, and so he goes to Galilee, a somewhat safer and better administered region. Matthew's two previous texts referred to definite prophecies; he refers to 'the prophet' in relation to the first, 'the prophet Jeremiah' for the second. This third time his reference is more general: 'So was fulfilled what was said through the prophets: "He will be called a Nazarene"'. None of the commentators has a clue about the origin of this prophecy. Possibly it is a pun on the word 'Nazareth', but where it comes from is obscure. But its very obscurity gives us a clue, I think, to the meaning of what Matthew is doing. What are we to make of this apparently artificial appeal to Scripture?

Matthew's practice is different from that of the other New Testament authors. While they often allude to Scripture without making much of it, he makes quite definite references. And he has a particular purpose in mind, as we can see if we compare his practice with the other Gospel that tells us of Jesus' conception and birth. In his account of the birth and early days of Jesus, Luke produces a series of prophets and prophecies – the Magnificat, Nunc Dimittis, and so on. Matthew's equivalent is to punctuate his story with references to Scripture. In their different ways these two writers are doing precisely the same thing: bringing out the significance of the great thing that was happening, though to all eyes but those of faith it is no more significant than any other birth. It is likely that by the time Matthew wrote, the first Christians would have begun to develop a collection of Old Testament texts which seemed to them significant in bringing out the meaning of Jesus' life, death and resurrection. Indeed, he may be drawing on the reference to the Nazarene in a quite conventional way, simply taking it from the current book of sermon illustrations.

And that takes me to the second point. For the New Testament writers, Scripture meant what we call the Old Testament. It was all they had until their writings in turn were accepted into what we have come to call the Bible, the Book. And their unanimous view was that the Old Testament as a whole spoke of Jesus, the one who was to come. One crucial text is from another Gospel, that of Luke, and it concerns the journey to Emmaus on the evening of the first Easter day. The companion of the two dispirited travellers, the risen Jesus as he is later revealed to be, chides them for their lack of faith. 'And beginning with Moses and all the prophets, he explained to them what was said in all the scriptures concerning himself' (Lk. 24.27). 'In all the scriptures . . .'. Paul is similar, and in 1 Corinthians 15, summarizing the gospel teaching, he twice uses the expression, 'according to the scriptures'. The second of those uses, with reference to the resurrection, has caused similar puzzlement to that of Matthew on the Nazarene. Where does Scripture foretell the resurrection?

But that takes us back to the point about not trying to prove too much. There is no definite prediction of the resurrection. But Scripture's prophecies are not to be treated as exact predictions of what is going to happen. Sometimes, indeed, they are: that Jerusalem would fall, and the people be taken into exile, for example. The New Testament has a broader concern, to show that as a whole, it is fulfilled by the coming of this child into the world. The power of God is shown in his freedom to make what he will of things: to surprise us in the way in which he does make things take place, in the unexpected way in which prophecy is fulfilled.

> Who would
> think, despite derision, that a child could lead the way?
> God surprises
> earth with heaven, coming here on Christmas Day.

Prophecy and Proof

The key to both Matthew's use of scripture and the meaning of the child with whom we have to do is the God made known in the pages of Scripture, from the first of them to the last, from the garden to the city of gold.

III

Though to all eyes but those of faith this is no more significant than any other birth, it is with the eyes of faith that we are concerned. It cannot be any other, because this is a warrior armed not with weapons of steel but with the power of the Word of God alone. If this is God among us, it is God incognito, God made man, and not one who is obviously divine. We should expect the same of his Old Testament anticipations. Only with hindsight, with the eyes provided by the God who raised Jesus from the dead, can we recognize the Suffering Servant of Isaiah – the one of whom we heard in our reading – as the one who was to come. It is quite likely, to say the least, that the prophet was referring to one nearer to his own time, possibly to Israel herself, in these remarkable prophecies. But because Jesus saw in them a model for his own manner of life and death, we can see that in fact, in God's providential ordering of things, they refer to him.

It was in the light of what they knew about Jesus that the first theologians saw all kinds of anticipations of Jesus in the Old Testament. Who was it that walked in the garden in the cool of the day, to challenge Adam and judge his sin? It was the Son of God, the one who was to become man in Jesus, so that Irenaeus can say that it was Jesus who walked there and accompanies Noah on the ark, and so on. The same could be said about all kinds of other places where the Old Testament showed God as becoming present and active in the world. Matthew is, in his own distinctive way, doing that: showing that the texts to which he appeals help us to make sense of the flight into Egypt, the slaughter of the innocents, and the fact that Jesus lived in so unfashionable a place as Nazareth. And in that way they show us the kind of saviour with whom we have to deal.

This is an odd kind of proof, is it not? How then are we to demonstrate to the world that the gospel is for all nations and peoples? We point to a man on a cross and that takes me to the other important point that needs to be made. The man on the cross is one kind of proof. But there is another person in the frame whom we must not neglect. I spoke about the fact that texts like Isaiah 49 are part of God's providential preparation for the coming of Christ. Isaiah may not have had Jesus of Nazareth in mind; but God the Father did. Why can we believe that? It is because, as the creed puts it, the Holy Spirit, 'spoke through the prophets' – that is, through the Old Testament texts which Matthew is using. He can use them in the way that he does because he believes that they are the work of God's Spirit, who enables the prophets to prepare the way and enables the apostles to interpret for us the meaning of the Christ child. The gospel, says Paul in our other reading, 'has now been revealed by the Spirit to God's holy prophets and apostles' (Eph. 3.5). It is because we believe in God the Spirit that we can gladly accept Matthew's appeal to these apparently odd texts from the Old Testament.

That leaves us with a final question about our part in the matter. How is the gospel to be made known to all nations and peoples of the earth? What is for us the message of Epiphany? Two points can be made. The first is that by his Spirit, God calls a community of worship and faith to be organized around the life, death and resurrection of his Son, Jesus. The existence and life of the church, warts and all, is God's dispensation for bringing the knowledge of his love to the peoples of the world. Epiphany leads us to mission, our being sent with a message of love and judgement to the world in which we live. And that means that a joyful and solemn task is laid upon us, to organize our life here so that others may learn with us to know Jesus and the Father who sent him. To put it in the terms with which I began the sermon, we do not have to prove too much because it is the Spirit who does the proving – otherwise there is no hope for us. Our mission is what we are given to do, difficult though it may be to know quite what it involves at any given time. We rely on the promise that the one who spoke through the prophets is now sent by the Father to empower our work and witness through the one who was born to Mary.

The second point is equally important. Although we are given a task, it does not depend on us for its completion; it really does not. The Spirit is indeed promised to the church, but he is also the Spirit who is active in all creation, who hovered over the waters of creation and sent those mysterious Magi to worship at the manger. We are sent into a world in which God is already at work, where he has purposed 'to bring all things in heaven and on earth together under one head, even Christ'.

12

Eternal Punishment

God's gifts and his call are irrevocable.

(Rom. 11.29)

EPIPHANY, 4 JANUARY 1998

Readings: Mic. 5.1–5; Rom. 11.25–36

I

Recently, I got into conversation on the train with someone who had been brought up in a Christian church – the denomination I had better not mention – but had rejected the God she had been presented with. It was clearly a rather harsh, all-determining God, I suspect rather keen on sending a large number of people to hell – very different from the God of love with whom Charles[1] presented us last Sunday. And here is another example of the same thing. I have a student part of whose study follows a similar theme: how is it that for generations it was taught that when the godly go to heaven, they will enjoy watching the damned suffering the torments of hell? Does our God, the God of the Bible, really encourage us to be like that? Next month, we are at my college to have some lectures, given by a different lecturer each year – this year by the Director of the National Gallery – in honour of the Victorian theologian, F. D. Maurice. And why were they instituted? As an act of reparation, because Maurice was dismissed from his post for questioning the doctrine of eternal punishment. (You are more likely to be dismissed nowadays for teaching it!)

---

1 Charles Steynor, member of Brentwood URC.

I could give a very long lecture on the reasons why such deeply problematic and offensive pictures of God have emerged in the Christian tradition, but will spare you that. Rather, I want to say a little about the topic being studied in Junior Church this month: what is our God like? There is no more important question, because what we worship, what we value above all, makes us the kind of people we are. At this epiphany season I might point it in this way: what kind of God is it that sends a group of foreign astrologers to visit a Jewish baby? What kind of God has the first patriarch Abraham blessed by gifts of bread and wine by a foreign king, indeed, one worshipping a pagan deity? These questions show that whatever else we do, we must never oversimplify. This is at the very least a God who behaves in unexpected ways. There are other peculiarities to be taken into account as well. Doesn't this God go about things in rather a strange way? As the verse goes, 'How odd of God to choose the Jews'. How odd of God to come as a baby in a crib, an apparently defeated prophet on a cross.

However odd those things may be, they make one thing clear. This God is known in *particular* actions: he sends Abraham, not somebody else; he comes in Jesus, not Barabbas or the Emperor Augustus or Adolf Hitler. But this leads to another question that further focuses our question about the kind of God with whom we have to do. Is he fair? First God chooses the Jews and then seems to reject them. He seems to call some people into his church, and not others. Should he not choose us all? Does he want to save only a few, consigning the rest to a kind of cosmic rubbish dump, as for so long it was taught? This God seems to have something to answer for. Now, I would not have raised the question in this way were it not a properly biblical question to raise. Indeed, it was raised by Paul the Apostle, particularly in his great Letter to the Romans, which is all about that very matter. One of the reasons why this letter is so involved and complicated is that Paul is trying to make sense of the whole, while at the same time taking all the details into account. What is God doing in history, with his apparent choosings and rejectings? Is he fair, or even consistent? To adapt one of Paul's own images, is not this God rather like a potter who makes one pot only to throw it against a wall and then make another? How do we make sense of the odd ways in which this God seems to work out his purposes?

II

Paul has two beliefs which he wants to defend. God is good, and God is consistent. Let us look at the latter first. 'God's gifts and his call are irrevocable.' When God does something, it stays done. Those words, from Romans 11.29, sum up much of what this apparently complicated letter is about. All three of the translations I looked at speak of God's 'gifts' here, though the word is sometimes rendered directly into English as 'charismata'. One commentator translates our verse: 'God does not go back on his acts of grace'. Paul is arguing that though it may appear that God does have something to answer for, does appear to be inconsistent, the way things have happened show the reverse, that he is reliable and consistent.

What, then, are the 'gifts' that Paul is speaking of? They are two in particular: the call of Israel and the calling of the Gentiles into the church through the life, death and resurrection of Jesus. The trouble is that they seem to be incompatible. First it seems as if the Jews rather than the Gentiles are called; then that once the Gentiles are in, the Jewish people are out. And that is a problem, for it makes it appear that God's promise to the Jews has failed. Isn't the fact that the Jews appear to have rejected the Gospel a sign that God has had to change his mind, that having tried one way he is now forced to try another? Israel has failed, so try the church instead? If that were so, Paul believes, God would have failed. But, 'God's gifts and his call are irrevocable'.

Now, I cannot go into all the complications of Paul's argument here, but shall restrict myself to the concern with which

I began. What kind of God do we meet here? Paul's argument is concerned with justice, not justice in the restricted sense we often use today, to refer to little more than a fairer share of material wealth, or seeing that the wicked are punished. Let me try to explain what I mean by comparing a narrower and broader sense of justice. The narrower sense can be explained by a simple example. The old doctrine of hell had, and perhaps has, a measure of justice in it. It does seem fair that those who have been unrepentantly wicked should meet with punishment in the end. In Mozart's great opera, the statue of the man he had murdered returns to drag Don Giovanni down to hell – though only after he had first demanded that he repent. That is dramatically right, as it is right that mass murderers and those who make the lives of others a misery should at least be shown the consequences of their crimes, even though most Christians do not now believe that they will be punished for ever. The punishment of the wicked is a kind of justice.

But that is not what Paul means by justice. If that were the only justice there were, if we received only our deserts, who could stand? Paul knows that none of us has the right to boast, none to be sure that what we do does not merit divine punishment. But God's justice, as it is shown in Jesus, does not remain at that level. God's justice is to be seen in the fact that the old law of punishment does not have the last word, but rather that everything possible is done to see that all are given a way to share the goodness of God. One way of putting this – and it would be only half right – would be to say that God's love is stronger than his justice. Far better is it to say that God's justice is his love in action, not punishing the wicked but taking upon himself the consequences of their evil in order to call them back to him. That is the fundamental reason for saying that God is good.

But is he consistent? In the passage we have heard, Paul concludes that Israel is at present disobedient to the heavenly call only for a purpose: to enable the Gentiles to come in. But the end in view, God's justice, will be realized when all belong in the one kingdom of glory, Jew and Gentile alike. We don't know when or how this will happen, only that God's past goodness, his sending of Jesus, is a guarantee that his renewing justice will prevail. In the gift of his Son, the Jewish Messiah, in some mysterious way, all will be called into God's kingdom, whoever and whatever they are. Whether and how far we can refuse, whether any will end up excluded – whether we can choose to go to hell rather than accept God's gifts – is another question and part of the mystery of human freedom. But the dominating message is this: that all human beings are created to share the love and the mercies of God, and God's consistency, goodness and justice are demonstrated by his actions enabling this to take place.

III

'God's gifts and his call are irrevocable.' The astrologers, the wise men, that mysterious figure Melchizedek – all of them foreigners – are part of God's way of bringing it about that all should be called to share in God's purposes of love. Epiphany is about God's universal justice, his bringing it about that without diminishment of our freedom, all are called to his purposes of grace and mercy. It is about opening up those gifts and that call to everyone, whoever they are, however sunk in depravity, evil and unbelief. That is why what Luther said at the beginning of the Reformation is so important: God's justice does not mean that action by which he punishes the evil-doer, but by which he justifies, brings back to him, the godless. God's justice *means* God seeing to it that all are called to share his mercies. That is the kind of God with whom we have to do.

What kind of God? Karl Barth said of his great predecessor Calvin that things might have been somewhat different if he had more often taken seriously his belief that God does truly meet us in Jesus of Nazareth. But it is not only a fault in Calvin. The tragedy of Christian history is that so often we have not put Jesus Christ at the centre of our thinking about God, that we do not use that stern and loving man, the one willing to go to death for us all, as the lens through which to view our God. 'He who has seen me has seen the Father.' The Father is one whose justice consists not in sending the wicked to hell but in going to the final limits to prevent our making hell for ourselves. The point is this: how can one who is prepared to love us, even to death, wish that any of his creation should finally perish? It can be put even more strongly: God through his Son endures the very pains of hell that we should be freed from them. 'God's gifts and his call are irrevocable.'

There can only be one response, and Paul makes it at the end of this remarkable argument: 'Oh, the depth of the riches of the wisdom and knowledge of God! How unsearchable his judgements, and his paths beyond tracing out . . . For from him and through him and to him are all things. To him be glory for ever! Amen'.

13

Secular and Divine Power

Worthy is the lamb who was slain, to receive power and wealth
and wisdom and might and honour and glory and blessing.
(Rev. 5.12)

1 April 2001

Readings: Exod. 6.2–13; Jn 11.45–53; Rev. 5.11–14

I

I have an acquaintance, a Catholic priest, whose father was an unbelieving Oxford don. He once asked him how much of the creed he could believe, and he thought about it and answered, 'Suffered under Pontius Pilate'. There will be some who will be sceptical about even that, but the fact is that this appears to be the most rock hard of all the articles which Christians confess. Yet its meaning is not so obvious. Much depends on who Pilate was and what his action means for the gospel story. So, first, something about Pilate. He was an official of the Roman Empire, and something must be said about that first. I have been reading a biography of Lord Curzon, perhaps the greatest viceroy of India under the British Empire. Two good things marked his rule. The first was his support of the Indian people against the administration in London; he really was someone who believed that his calling was to serve the interests of his charges. And the second was his irritation when people were appointed because they had contacts with the government. An aristocrat himself, he got where he did by his sheer ability, interestingly enough the only one of a very old family to make any real impact outside the sheep fields of

Derbyshire. Government jobbery he could not stand. And that is where his attitude, and the organization of the British Empire in general, stands in marked contrast with that of Rome, which was almost totally ruthless and exploitative. 'They make a wilderness and call it peace', as a famous German rebel claimed. (I don't know if any of you grow the rather insipid rose called 'Peace', but I once heard that described in the same terms by a gardening broadcaster.) Pilate got where he did by his contacts more than his ability and played no notable part in anything – except for this.

He had, to be sure, one of the very worst jobs in the empire. The Jews were quite intransigent, unique in the Roman Empire for their absolute refusal to lie down under oppression. Or at least some of them were. The situation can be compared with the behaviour of the Christians under Russian Communism. The Orthodox church tended to cooperate with the regime; Baptists tended to go to jail for their faith. Similarly, there were all kinds of Jewish attitudes to Roman rule, ranging from cooperation to outright military rebellion. The various groups Jesus is recorded as encountering – Pharisees, Zealots, Sadducees – all had different attitudes. It was the intransigent ones who won the argument in the end, if it is a victory to have rebelled and to have their land completely destroyed in the years after Jesus' death. Despite their differences, the Jews almost all shared one thing. They were unique in that alone of the many peoples of the empire they refused to allow their faith in the one God to be compromised by combining their faith with the many gods of Roman religion. The Romans allowed this, but were always uneasy, and for good reasons. Revolt could, and did, break out at any time, and it is not surprising that Pilate was jumpy. In Jesus, he feared that he met not just a religious teacher, but one who would set fire to the whole nation.

II

All that provides the background to our text. We heard in our first reading the story of how the chief priests conspired to have Jesus executed, bringing about in ways they never expected his death for the whole world. The story is presented in the ironical way John loves, showing as he does that God brings about his purposes through the decisions of others who think they are doing something quite different. The authorities think they are sacrificing Jesus for the peace of the nation; and they achieve the salvation of the world. John makes a similar point in recounting a later episode, when Jesus is on trial for his life, before Pilate. He records, in his unique fashion, the way in which he understands the encounter between two powerful men, one seeming to be powerful, the other in fact holding all the cards. Jesus is in his own way as intransigent as a Zealot, first refusing to answer one question and then answering another in a way that must have surprised the governor. 'Pilate said, "Don't you realize that I have power either to free you or to crucify you?". "You would have no authority at all over me," Jesus replied, "if it had not been granted you from above"' (Jn 19.10b–11a).

The first thing to note is how ordinary is this scene. The same kind of encounter happens again and again in our world. It is an encounter between what used to be called a hanging judge and an apparently miserable offender in the dock. Further, Pilate is an ordinary man, and I can predict that in the same situation most of us would have behaved in roughly the same way. Rulers have to keep order; if they do not, their authority disappears, and they are replaced by someone else. Indeed, it is their job to keep order, that their subjects might be free to live peaceful and godly lives. Later in the scene, Jesus recognizes this: 'he who handed me over to you has the greater sin'. So the scene is pretty ordinary at many levels. Public order must be maintained, and mere matters of justice cannot be allowed to stand in the way.

But at another level what is going on is not at all ordinary. A titanic power struggle is being waged. And, although Pilate does not realize it, all the power lies with the prisoner. We may think that it is an encounter between a powerless man and the representative of the greatest empire the world had so far known. It is in fact a battle between a weak time-server and the only real power the world has over it, even if it does not recognize it. John indicates this with his usual gift for the double meaning. Pilate's power comes only 'from above'. He probably takes this to mean: from Rome, from the source of his worldly authority, which Rome was in due time to take from him. But Jesus knows better. There is no power that is not exercised through God's gift or permission. We shall come in a moment to think about what this means for our celebration of Passion Sunday, but first let me illustrate from another book of Scripture, another book written by a John, although very likely a different one.

The Book of Revelation is also about a power struggle, fought and won on the cross of Jesus, between the power of God and the power of the mighty Roman Empire. The writer shows us something that our Gospel does not, that the events happening on earth are also and at the same time eternal events, events happening in heaven, the place from which God rules the earth. The encounter between Jesus and Pilate is also something that is going on in the eternal realm. That is why Jesus is the one with the power in his hands. Revelation is giving us a God's-eye view of that which John sees from the point of view of Jesus and Pilate. He therefore shows us who this truly is who stands, wearing the mocking crown of thorns, before the viceroy's throne. There is a vision of a rider on a white horse: 'his name is faithful and true . . . and he was called the Word of God'. That is why he has the power given from above; he is that power in action upon earth. 'On his robe and on his thigh was written the title, "King of kings and Lord of lords"' (Rev. 19.16). The increasingly lonely, rejected and apparently ordinary figure on his way to a brutal death is 'King of kings and Lord of lords', to whom Pilate could do nothing unless it were given to him from above to do it.

III

What are we to make of the fact that Jesus suffered under Pontius Pilate? How do we approach the celebration of the

Secular and Divine Power

run-up to Easter? There are two popular responses which I believe both to be wrong. One was fashionable in years gone by, and still now to an extent; the other is a very modern response. The first, those of you who visited the Seeing Salvation exhibition at the National Gallery will have witnessed: devotion to Jesus is seen in much of our artistic tradition as a kind of sympathy with his sufferings, so that our preparation for Easter involves trying to get into his mind and suffering. But if John is right, that is not what it is about. Jesus himself will have none of it: 'Weep not for me but for your children', as he told one group of sympathizers. We are the ones who need the sympathy, for what is going on is a human joining of the wrong side, the side that is going to lose. Like the disciples in another account of the same event, our attitude should be one of astonished awe at the majesty of this man's authority. He really is in charge. He needs not our sympathy but our faith.

The other mistaken approach is to see the sympathy going the other way: that on the cross we have God suffering alongside us, showing that although the world is a mess, he shares the mess with us. God, in the words of one rather wet philosophy, is the fellow sufferer who understands. Well he is not, or at least not primarily that. He is the sovereign God revealed in Jesus' demeanour before Pilate. If we listen to John, we shall realize that Jesus' suffering is first of all an act of divine power. John shows us this in the way he tells the story. Jesus insists that he is laying down his life of his own free will. Only when he chooses will the authorities be able to arrest and kill him. Verse 7.30: 'They tried to seize him, but no one could lay hands on him, because his appointed hour had not yet come'. Jesus' suffering is an act of power, of sovereign divine power, which nothing is able to resist. All the Gospels have their particular ways of showing that this is not only God's sovereign act. It is that of Jesus, too. He is in charge and does freely that which he has been sent to do.

We can put this another way. 'Suffered under Pontius Pilate' is an article of the creed, the document which tells the story of salvation, the document which is the marching orders of the church. God does not sympathize with us; that is only for those who can do nothing else about the situation. Here is not a passable deity, but Lord of all authority and rule. In Jesus he shares our life in order to make all things new. We can see this illustrated at the most ordinary level. Remember the lines of the hymn, 'All the light of sacred story / gathers round its head sublime'.[1] Not merely sacred story, but all the stories ever told take their meaning from this ordinary event. There simply is no one like this, even at the most obvious level that no one act has changed the world to the degree that this one has.

We are given a share in that power, though our power is only that of Jesus, the power of the word and of suffering. Sometimes a word is enough. As Luther famously said of the Devil, a word shall quickly slay him. The story is told of the Russian Christian philosopher Nicholas Berdyaev being hauled up before Russia's Marxist rulers. He simply looked them in the eye, as Jesus looked at Pilate, and told them that he simply did not accept the basis of their authority. They did not kill him – there he was unusual – but expelled him from the country, a bad enough fate for any Russian. The Gospel gave him power to resist, and he did. It involved suffering for him, and for many Russian Christians much more. We know at least part of the outcome of their struggle, and it is again illustrated by the book of Revelation. The real power on earth is that exercised by the martyrs, those who witness to and perhaps die for their faith.

Such ultimate sacrifices may not be required of us; pray that they may not. Yet the basis of our life on earth is just the same. 'Suffered under Pontius Pilate.' This apparently ordinary, easily believable, statement of fact is the key to all of our life on earth: that through his stripes we are healed and set free to rule on earth through the Gospel we have to live and to proclaim.

---

1   *Rejoice and Sing*, 224.

14

Jesus, the Second Adam

At once, the Spirit drove him out into the wilderness, and there he remained for forty days, tempted by Satan. He was among the wild beasts, and the angels attended to his needs.

(Mk 1.12–3)

4 March 2001

Readings: Gen. 3.17–24; Mk 1.4–13; Rom. 5.12–17

I

To be human is to be given a task to perform, humble or great or simply routine. No life is pointless, however much some people come to think that theirs is. We are all needed for something and certainly for somebody – or more likely somebodies. Of course, in all that, we are very different from one another. Of one we say he is a driven man, of another that she sails through life untroubled. Yet common to us all is that we are created in the image of God and that means, among other things, that we are all given a task or series of tasks to perform. That is one of the points made by the story of Adam in the book of Genesis. He is given a garden to tend. The earth has to be made a home for the creatures God has put in it. When God says to his human creation in the first creation narrative, 'Fill the earth and subdue it', it is a responsible task, not an invitation to ruthless exploitation. It is, as the theologian Moltmann has said, to make of the earth a home.

But Adam fails, and he is driven from the garden. Having chosen what he thought was the easier option, he learns the hard way that it is not. He is driven out to make his living in somewhat less pleasant circumstances, a driven man in another sense of the word. Of course, this does not mean that God abandons him. Quite the opposite. He still has a task to perform, and what we call civilization takes shape through him and his descendants. But it is all now a struggle. Death has come into the world, not just physical death, but the fact that life is often so deadly, such a struggle and a weariness, like so much of our earthly labour. 'You will get food from [the earth] only by labour.'

Adam now does not have a garden to tend, but a wilderness to tame, not only outwardly but within himself. There are, we might say, wild beasts around him, and a wild beast within him to be tamed. But where does that lead us? You may remember that last time I said that I planned a number of sermons on what we call the Nicene Creed. As we come to Lent, we come naturally to the second Adam, and the confession, 'he was made man'. In the first instance, that refers to what we celebrate at Christmas. But Jesus' humanity is far more than that, and so today we think of an episode in his career without which we cannot understand his humanity – and that means also our own – at all. Let us then look at some verses from Mark (1.12–13): 'At once, the Spirit drove him out into the wilderness, and there he remained for forty days, tempted by Satan. He was among the wild beasts, and the angels attended to his needs'.

II

At the beginning of his ministry, Jesus goes to be baptized by the Old Testament prophet, John. John preaches repentance, and Jesus joins Israel in confessing their joint responsibility in the failure of all mankind, for sharing in the sin of Adam. The Holy Spirit descends upon him, anointing him for his particular task in life, and God reveals that it is a very special task indeed. 'You are my beloved Son; in you I take delight.' That almost certainly links Jesus with Israel, sometimes called God's son in Scripture, the son who had failed him. Here is a true son of Adam and of Israel in whom God can indeed delight. But it is by no means plain sailing, as they say, after that. What does it mean to be a son in whom the Father delights? That has to be worked out. He has to learn obedience through what happens to him. And so we come to an extremely odd episode, full of biblical symbolism and suggestions, which Mark describes rather more briefly than the accounts we usually hear.

The writer uses a word we have heard a number of times already. 'At once, the Spirit drove him out into the wilderness, and there he remained for forty days, tempted by Satan. He was among the wild beasts, and the angels attended to his needs.' Another driven man. Some commentators call attention to the violence which may be suggested in that account. 'The Spirit *drove* him out.' Having heard God's affirmation of him, he is *immediately* – one of Mark's favourite words – sent for a test. As Adam is driven into the wilderness, so Jesus is driven into the wilderness to be tempted, to face the wild beasts without and within. Who else had had a similar experience? Israel, who spent forty years – a Hebrew expression for a long period – in the wilderness, being tested and tempting God in their turn. Those of you who are familiar with the worship of the *Book of Common Prayer* will know well the words of Psalm 95, 'Do not be stubborn, as you were at Meribah, as on that day at Massah in the wilderness, when your forefathers made trial of me, tested me, though they had seen what I did'. Like Adam, like Israel, after Adam and after Israel, this man is sent vigorously and without delay by the Spirit of his Father into the wilderness to be tempted. But unlike them, he comes out unscathed. He is indeed the son whom God loves.

The great Congregationalist theologian John Owen pointed out that this was not the only temptation Jesus experienced. Indeed, the whole of his life was a testing – through the trials of those who opposed him, through Peter's temptation that he should not be a suffering Messiah, through the final testing in Gethsemane and the cross. 'If you are the Son of God, come down from the cross', as his mockers tempt. What does it all mean? 'Ours is not a high priest unable to sympathize with our weaknesses, but one who has been tested in every way as we are, only without sinning' (Heb. 4.15). It is not that he experienced the same temptations as we do. As I have said, we all have particular callings in life, and the temptations tend to go with them. As I have also sometimes said, academics are characteristically tempted to arrogance and to despise those who seem less clever, less accomplished, while Jesus' temptations flowed from the kind of calling that he had. Like Adam, he is tempted to take the easy way, to power, popularity, celebrity. (Now there's a lesson for our time!)

The point is twofold: first, that even this man's achievement was not without labour, and certainly not automatic; and second that his Father sends his messengers the angels and his Spirit to support and lead him in his way and, unlike Adam, he obeys; but the price is high, indeed, the highest. It seems likely that here Mark is indicating what Paul was later to make explicit, that here is the second Adam, the one who walks upright when the other stumbles and falls. As Irenaeus said in one of the most brilliant images of all theology, Jesus recapitulates the life of Adam, goes over again its main stages from life, through maturity, to death, lives out the same story, but this time triumphantly. And so we return to Adam, to see something of what he might mean for us.

III

The story of Adam is a most interesting and revealing one, permanently interesting, because it tells us so much about ourselves. But we are not interested in it for itself. Indeed, to be interested only in it, in all the silly jokes about the apple – which, incidentally, it was not, but simply a fruit – can be

Jesus, the Second Adam

positively unhealthy. There is no doubt that the traditional doctrine of original sin has sometimes cast too negative a light on human beings, because it has been treated too much on its own, apart from the second Adam's achievement. We only know what Adam means in the light of what the man Jesus, the eternal Son of God in flesh, achieved to right that which was wrong. We only know the meaning of sin through its overcoming on the cross, only know our need in the light of its overcoming. We make our prayer of confession Sunday by Sunday as those who are loved and forgiven, not as those who must grovel in the dirt to prove their unworthiness. We are unworthy, but made worthy through his life, death and resurrection.

Here, there are two things to be said. On the one hand, because of what Jesus has done we do not have to earn our worthiness, our acceptance by God. That great writer whom we have already met, the author of the letter to the Hebrews, is quite definite about that. This man's life, won through trial, temptation and suffering, is a new and living way into the presence of God. Because he has gone before us, the author and pioneer of our faith, we can simply trust in his life, his work, his cross. 'Nothing in my hands I bring; simply to thy cross I cling.'[1] We are made holy through his death, made clean, brought before God not in our own rags, but, as Calvin liked to put it, clothed in Christ's righteousness. ('Reclothe us in our rightful mind.'[2]) And this is something that holds throughout our life. The one who won his way through trial and temptation is still and for ever the one who intercedes for us before the throne of grace.

But, and this is the second point, it does not follow that it will be easy. After Adam, our life has to be worked out in what we call real life with all its trials and temptations. If we have to follow Jesus, who would expect anything else? Here I think

---

1 *Rejoice and Sing*, 365.
2 *Rejoice and Sing*, 492.

that we have to distinguish between two things that are quite close. God himself does not tempt us. It is the Devil who tempts Jesus, and however we are to understand that, we know the kind of thing that is meant. There is an inner voice telling us: just one will not matter; nobody will know; why should I be too strict with myself; and so on. You and I know all too well how it works, and how so much of modern advertising and our consumer ideology is designed to work on us in that way also. These temptations do not come from God; they come from our inheritance as children of Adam. And yet it does not follow that God does not test us. Some of the great figures of Scripture who are set up as examples for us are tested, not as some might torture animals or men for a kind of perverted pleasure but to find out what kind of mettle we are made of and to enable us to grow. Abraham and Job are famous among them. Does Abraham really trust God, so as to accept that he must sacrifice the son in whom all his hopes lie? Does Job fear God for naught? They are truly great figures because they trust, and because they show us that no one trusts in God and is confounded. Without trial, we do not grow, and much of the point of the life of faith is that we continue to grow, in grace and in the love of one another and our neighbour. What a trial – as we say – that can often be. 'To live above.' Yet the angels saw to Jesus' needs, and God through his Spirit will see to ours too. Even, perhaps especially, our trials carry that promise.

But there is something even more wonderful to be said about this story, and it comes from another great theologian of our tradition, John Milton, a contemporary of John Owen. As *Paradise Lost* moves towards its conclusion, the archangel Michael speaks to Adam and Eve as they are about to be driven out of Eden and tells them of the one who is to come, Jesus. Adam loses his composure as he hears these mysteries. He exclaims:

Jesus, the Second Adam

> O Goodness infinite, goodness immense!
> That all this good of evil shall produce,
> And evil turn to good.[3]

There is an ancient Latin tag, which speaks of the happy fault that merited such a redeemer. We must beware of it, for it might suggest that evil is justified by its overcoming. We can never justify evil, but we can with Milton rejoice that the coming of the second Adam almost justified the sin of the first, because of its overwhelming blessing.

> Much more good thereof shall spring
> to God more glory, more good will to men
> From God, and over wrath grace shall abound.[4]

As we heard in the reading from Romans, 'God's act of grace is out of all proportion to Adam's wrongdoing . . . If by the wrongdoing of one man, death established its reign . . . how much more shall those who in far greater measure receive grace and the gift of righteousness live and reign through the one man, Jesus Christ'. 'Over wrath grace shall abound.' We learn today that grace abounds because of the wearying and finally deadly life lived by the eternal Son of God who was made man for our salvation.

---

3 Milton, *Paradise Lost*, Book 12, ll. 469–71.
4 Milton, *Paradise Lost*, Book 12, ll. 476–8.

15

Prophecy

> Write, therefore, what you have seen, what is now, and what will take place later.
>
> (Rev. 1.19)

10 December 2000

Readings: Hab. 1.12—2.3; Rev. 1.9–19

I

There was, in the news last week, a prediction that we are in for a continuation throughout the winter of the wet and windy weather we have been experiencing of late. And I thought, that probably means that it will be dry and clear. We have become sceptical about secular prophecy, especially about the weather, and I only have to be told by the scientists that we are going to live longer and longer lives to wonder where the next great plague is coming from. Just think for a minute about modern prophecy, or futurology as it is sometimes called. On the one hand, we have the predictions of the astrologers, carefully formulating their horoscopes so that whatever happens they will be proved to be right. Prophecy as vacuousness, we might say. On the other hand, there are the pseudo-scientific prophets, those who latch on to some recent development and project it into the future. Usually, this kind of prophecy assumes that the future will be more of the same, more of what we are now experiencing. And, if you look back on what has happened, they have usually been wrong. What actually happens is generally unpredictable. Another important point here was made by a recent writer, that science fiction, as it is called, is the literature of atheism. It is prophecy of and for an age that has forsaken belief in God, so that it is human or 'alien' beings that call the tune not the God of Israel and Jesus. In science fiction we meet the prophecy of unbelief.

Prophecy is, however, an old and respectable calling, at least in parts of the Bible's witness. There were false prophets, so that those we call the prophets sometimes felt it necessary to distance themselves from the professionals. ('I was not a prophet or a son of a prophet, but I was a shepherd', Amos 7.14.) The true prophets were not professionals, spin doctors serving for profit, but heard things straight from the mouth of the Lord. For the most part, prophecy was a noble and persecuted calling, men so determined to tell the truth about the human condition that they sometimes suffered unspeakable pains for their honesty.

When we think of biblical prophecy, we think mainly of the Old Testament, those great men who called Israel back to her responsibilities and produced those mysterious promises which were fulfilled in Jesus. But the New Testament has a great tradition of prophecy, too. Paul recognizes it as among the gifts given to some members of his churches, while prophets have quite a part to play in the expansion of the church in the Acts of the Apostles. However, perhaps the greatest of the New Testament prophets is the writer of the book we know as Revelation.

It is a strange book and has sometimes been rejected as sub-Christian, inappropriate for Scripture. It appears to be violent and vengeful, and it is certainly full of sometimes horrific imagery; not, it seems, the product of an entirely balanced mind. But, of course, some ages call for this kind of treatment. When the times are apocalyptic, when all seems to be falling in ruin, a prophet is someone who helps to make sense of things. If we look carefully at one of the things written in this book, we shall, I hope, discover something of the meaning of this book and, at the same time, something of the two things which come together this evening: Scripture and our preparation for Christmas.

II

Like the prophets, John is summoned in a vision into the heavenly council. Like his predecessors, he is probably suffering for his witness, in exile on a small Greek island. And he is told to write his vision on a scroll: to produce a *scripture* for the churches in his care. He has a vision of the risen and ascended Jesus, and he describes him in language borrowed from Old Testament prophecy, and especially Daniel and Ezekiel. This is the risen Lord in glory. Notice the imagery of light: clothes of dazzling whiteness, 'and his eyes like blazing fire'. The vision is so overwhelming that John falls as though dead, but he is reassured, in some of the greatest words of Scripture: 'Do not be afraid. I am the first and the last, and the living one. I was dead, and behold I am alive for ever, and I hold the keys of death and death's domain'. And so we come to our text, and it again refers to Scripture: writing. 'Write, therefore, what you have seen, what is now, and what will take place later' (Rev. 1.19).

Notice the three tenses of what he is to write, the past, the present and the future: 'what you have seen, what is now, and what will take place later'. That is almost a summary of the prophet's calling – saying in words what is to be seen. Let us look at the three tenses one at a time. First there is the past tense: 'What you have seen'. What does John see that has happened? The worship of heaven, around the throne and the Lamb, praising God and his Christ, and for two things especially: the creation of the world and its redemption on the cross of Jesus. Chapters 4 and 5 of this book provide the prophetic bedrock, the foundation of everything for John. God has created and he has acted to save. There is also more, and to the very end our author celebrates God's past goodness. 'I saw the Holy City, coming down from heaven'; and a voice is heard, 'Behold, the dwelling of God is with men'. The city is an image for Jesus, who 'came down', who became flesh and dwelt among us at the first Christmas time. The creation, the crib and the cross. That is what the prophet shows us as the basis for what is now happening.

So we come to the present. And what is happening now? Suffering, persecution and martyrdom. That is what John sees happening to the tiny church in the midst of a mighty empire which is at odds with it and with God's will. All the imagery, repellent as it sometimes seems to us, is dedicated to showing that the church's suffering is more than it seems. It is not just the suffering of a tiny minority in the hands of an evil empire. It is simply one aspect of a battle going on in heaven, a battle which God has won on the cross, and will win. John wants to give his churches – and us with them – eyes to see what is really going on.

We are sometimes tempted to think that the world is falling apart, and perhaps in one sense it is. In our case, the empire is more subtle and hidden – the empire of money, of consumerism which sees only one end in view for its machinations: profit, even at the expense of breaking up families, encouraging societies to degenerate into competitive violence, anything so long as it aids the growth of wealth. There are plenty of allusions to the power of money in this book. It appears to be master, as it often does in our world. And yet John says that the one who really rules, whose empire will have no end, unlike all the earthly empires we so fear, is the lamb on his throne. John shows his suffering church that God's will is indeed done in heaven and is also done on earth so long as the church remains faithful to its Lord. We are not as powerless as we may think. The one whose eyes are like blazing fire is the first and the last and the living one. The book begins with him, proceeds to demonstrate his rule, even in the chaos of the Roman Empire, and ends with a promise that he will come again.

And that takes us to the future, to our third tense, 'what will take place later'. It is a mistake to take the book of Revelation, as the doorstep preachers so often do, as primarily concerned with details of what is going to happen in future time. It is mainly concerned to show that the one who was born and raised to everlasting life will have the last word on our world and on our lives. That is the only thing that this prophecy is finally concerned with. And it brings me to the point of all our talk of prophecy. Earlier, I said that in our world the prophecies of the astrologers and the writers of science fiction are mainly more of the same, despite the way it is often dressed up. True prophecy is, also, like all prophecy, more of the same. But it is its content that is entirely different.

For Scripture, the real past is not what we think it is, our human history of suffering and disaster, of human achievement, empire, war and all the rest. The past of prophecy is rather something stretching back far further than any history we can remember, and that is God's creating and redeeming love. The real present is not the scramble to get ready for Christmas day, although we shall all be involved in that, in different ways. The real present is that all our busyness is embraced by one who tells us to remember that there are other things, other priorities, than feeding the family and the profits of the banks. The real present is the Spirit's reminding us that, despite all, he is Lord, the one who came as man and died on the cross. And as for the future, it differs utterly from that of the astrologers and the futurologists. The real future is not the future in the stars, which are but lamps hung up in heaven by God, not the breeding of the superman of the evolutionists' dream, but the return of Christ in glory.

III

So much of our Christmas can be an evasion of the truth that we shall die, that our lives are marked by suffering and death. We often pray for those for whom this is a particularly difficult time of year, as indeed it is, simply because of the unreality of the expectations we impose upon it. We hope to shut out the world for a few days, but we cannot, or at least we cannot in the way we try to. We cannot shut it out, but we can embrace it by hope. That is John's message. Let us end by looking briefly at two of the verses with which this great book of prophecy comes to an end. We return to the vision in chapter 21 of the holy city, coming down to earth from heaven. Verse 3 refers to the first Christmas: 'Behold, the dwelling of God is with men'. In the next verse John shows us the real future: 'For he shall wipe away every tear from their eyes. There will be no more death or mourning or crying or pain, for the old order of things has passed away'. The old order has passed, it is passing, and, in the end, it will finally pass away, and there will be a new heaven and a new earth. That is prophecy. At Christmas, our suffering is embraced by hope, not by hope of ever more of the same, but of something far greater, something that will put into perspective all our suffering and expectations: the completion of that which began when the Son of God became man for us and our salvation.

16
Death and the Resurrection

> The sea gave up the dead that were in it, and Death and Hades gave up the dead in their keeping.
>
> (Rev. 20.13)

6 MAY 2001[1]

Readings: Dan. 12.1–10; Rev. 20.1–6, 11–15; Lk. 20.27–38

I

I begin for once by reading the text, because I shall probably not read it again until nearly the end: 'The sea gave up the dead that were in it, and Death and Hades gave up the dead in their keeping'.

Some time ago, at a conference in Oxford, I was walking past a famous old library with one of my research students and observed that the library was supposed to be haunted. Her comment was, but Christians cannot believe in ghosts. We don't believe in spirits, for according to Scripture, when you are dead, you are dead. There is nothing remaining over until the resurrection at the end of time. I believe that we have to take that very seriously and do not always do so at Christian funerals. Death is absolute and final, at least in one respect. Occasionally at funerals you hear things said, no doubt, in a quite proper attempt to comfort the bereaved, to suggest otherwise, like a dreadful verse that is sometimes heard suggesting that the person is not dead, but like someone sitting in the next room. That is quite contrary to Scripture's teaching and that of

---

1 This sermon was first preached exactly two years before Colin Gunton's death.

the creed: 'We look forward to the resurrection of the dead and the life of the world to come'. Two weeks ago Robert[2] preached about the impact of the resurrection faith on our life today. Today I want to say something about it in the context of Christian hope: 'We look forward'.

Before I come to look at our text, some general points about biblical teaching. First, unlike the Greeks, the Hebrews did not believe that we were made up of two separate pieces, a body and a soul, the latter of which flew off to heaven when we died. When Adam is created, he is a lump of clay into which God has breathed the breath or spirit of life. When that spirit departs, you are quite dead, food for the worms or carrion birds if left around. Of man as well as all the other creatures, it is said, 'when you take away their breath they die, and return to the dust'. 'It is not the dead who praise the Lord, not those who go down to the silent grave' (Ps. 115.17). The Old Testament, in particular, is insistent upon this, and only towards the end of the period is there even talk of a resurrection. And that takes me to the second point. The Bible speaks in terms of two ages at least as much as of two realms. While we speak of heaven as somewhere 'up there' to which the dead go, Scripture teaches for the most part that the resurrection is at the end of time; the dead must await it, and until that time they are simply dead. We speak of people being in heaven, but that is not for the most part the biblical teaching – though there are exceptions, as we shall see. You do not fly up to heaven when you die; you rot and await the resurrection in God's due time.

There is an important qualification to be made to this, and I shall come to it. But it is important at this stage that we do not evade the reality of death. As I often say, sometimes from here, I think that the church often fails in preparing people for death, as I have seen recently as several members of my family have died in extreme old age. A tale I heard recently indicates

---

2 Robert Canham, the minister at Brentwood URC at the time.

what has happened in our Western world, or part of it at any rate, suggesting that we are not prepared for death. It comes from one of the poorest downtown areas of America and concerns the difference between the way white and black people experience old age. The white people for the most part groan and moan, complain about their ills and the things they can no longer do. I suspect that we can see something of ourselves in that. The other group are quite different, rejoicing as they approach the time when they will be with God. They know that they are going to heaven and become the more joyful as they approach it. That may seem to contradict what I said earlier about the reality of death, but it still helps to make my point about our discomfort with the whole topic of death. As we come to the end of this introductory section, let me make the point again. For Scripture, death is not the escape of the soul upwards to heaven; it is a state in which the body decays in expectation of its renewal and resurrection in the life of the age to come. Until then, we remain dead . . . in expectation.

II

In the light of this, let me look at a famous chapter of Scripture, one of the most controversial and disputed in the history of the church, Revelation 20. It concerns the millennium, the so-called thousand-year reign of the saints before the end of the age. Next Wednesday, I am to examine a thesis written by an American student about a periodical which flourished for a few years in the 1820s and was called *The Morning Watch*. The journal was dedicated to propagating the teaching that the return of Jesus was imminent and, not only that, but that on his return true believers would reign with him on earth for a thousand years before the final end of all things. That pre-millenarianism, as it is called, is based on a wrong interpretation of Revelation 20. As we have heard, this chapter speaks of those 'who come to life and reign with Christ for a thousand years'. It is quite clear from the text who these are. They are the martyrs, those who have been killed for their witness to Jesus, 'the souls of those who had been executed for the testimony of Jesus and the Word of God' (Rev. 20.4). This is a heavenly, not an earthly reign. In other words, there is a two-stage resurrection. The first resurrection is that of the martyrs who, by virtue of what they have suffered, are rewarded by being raised with Christ in advance of everybody else. They do go straight to heaven, to reign with the Lord for whom they have laid down their lives. 'Blessed and holy are those who share in this first resurrection' (Rev. 20.6). And the thousand years is not to be taken literally, but is symbolic of the time between Jesus' resurrection and the end of all things at his return. They are, in John's eyes, the advance guard of the resurrection.

The remainder of the human race have to wait until the time when God will bring all our time and history to an end. John sees this happening in a vision of the great white throne and the One – God – who sits upon it. 'From his presence earth and heaven flew away.' Now we know from the next chapter that there are to be a new heaven and a new earth. But in this one, we hear something of what happens at the very end of human history. It is a scene of all human life standing before the throne of God the judge. 'I saw the dead, great and small, standing before the throne; and books were opened.' (Rather like the VAT inspector visiting a business and demanding an opening of the books, we might imagine.) The first thing that happens at the resurrection is, as the book of Daniel prophesied, the judgement of all. The record of every life is placed before the throne of the judge.

But then something else happens. Our deeds, what we have done in our lives, are not judged simply in their own light. If that were so, who could stand? Who could endure the searching sight of God who knows the secrets of all our hearts? And so a second book is brought forward, the book of life. As George Caird has observed, 'into the scale in men's favour are set the gracious, predestining purpose of God, and the redemptive love of him who died to ransom men for God'.[3] Remember that in Colossians Paul says that on the cross Christ cancelled the bond of debt that stood against us. At the resurrection our cause is pleaded by the one who lived and died for us. The record must be told; each life must be weighed in the balance. That is what the resurrection is about. But the old picture of some going to torment, others to heaven is quite unbalanced, for it forgets that our judge is the one who died for us, and his judgement will be gentle. The only persons who are actually named as being destroyed in the lake of fire are Death and Hades. There may be others, but that is left to the gracious judgement of God. For those who call on the name of God and his Christ, however, the resurrection is not half threat and half promise, but promise: promise that our faults and weaknesses will be purged away and the worn-out bodies in which we go into the realm of death will be transformed into the life of the age to come.

III

I began the first section of the sermon with a reference to the fact that while Greek philosophy tends to speak of a body and soul, the latter of which goes off to heaven at our death, the biblical tradition speaks rather of the whole person, a body animated by the spirit that God gives and takes away. The book of Revelation makes that clear: the record books hold what we have done with our lives, as the bodily human beings which we are. But I also suggested that the belief in heaven has a positive and Christian function. It enables us to look forward to death positively. Should we speak of people as going to be with God after they die? Does it undermine the biblical belief in the resurrection? What is it to be dead? It is to have no sense of time, and so, from the point of view of the dead, the resur-

---

3 G. B. Caird, *A Commentary on the Revelation of St John the Divine* (London: A&C Black, 1966) p. 259.

rection will follow directly, even though from the point of view of those still living, our dead are in the hands of death awaiting final redemption. To die is to go into God's eternal realm, the realm where he rules.

The important point, however, is this. If Jesus is the resurrection and the life, then our categories can no longer be understood rigidly. He is the resurrection now, and he will be it at the end. We don't have to worry about whether a thing happens now or whether we await it in the tomb. In his sermon two weeks ago, Robert rightly made much of the fact that we live something of the resurrection in the here and now. That is not in any way inconsistent with what our author is saying; in fact, in his very next chapter, he shows that the future resurrection bears upon life in the present. The fact that heaven and earth flee away is witness not to their abolition, but to their replacement with a new heaven and earth, the heaven and earth that are present wherever Jesus is and is proclaimed by his church.

Yet the new heaven and new earth await their full consummation in the return of Christ and the resurrection of the dead. Rehearsing during the past few weeks Verdi's great *Requiem*, I have been more and more convinced that the traditional requiem is badly out of balance, just like our traditional pictures of the last judgement. Verdi wonderfully expresses its teaching: *dies irae*: day of wrath; *lacrymosa* – full of tears will that time be. But it is one-sided – or, rather, it is two-sided when it ought to be one-sided. There is indeed a threat: into the lake of fire are flung 'those whose names were not to be found in the book of life'. But ours are found there, we can be confident, and maybe it is in the eternal purposes of God to save all of his human creatures at the last. We do not know and cannot really speculate. It is enough for us to know that for those who trust in God, and particularly in the redemption won for all mankind by Christ's cross, however weak and feeble our trust, the primary reality is one of rejoicing and gladness. That is why we should be able to look forward to our

Death and the Resurrection

death calmly and hopefully, joyfully even. I remember Malcolm Muggeridge answering the charge that Christians only believe in God because they are afraid of dying. It is rather the case, he said, exaggerating somewhat I fear, that Christians are the only ones who do not fear death. The promise of the resurrection does not take away the utter seriousness with which we live our lives; the records will be there. But our God is not a bookkeeper, like the splendid but tragic policeman Javert in *Les Misérables*. We shall be judged, but we shall be judged by the one who went through death and hell for us. Notice again the great promise in our chapter, and it is in the verse I have chosen for a text: 'Death and Hades gave up the dead in their keeping'. Those who die remain for a time in the earth in the hands of death, but at the last they will be raised, as was Jesus on the third day, the firstborn of many, the first-fruits of those who have fallen asleep.

17

Death and Modernity

Let no debt remain outstanding, except the continuing debt to love one another . . .

(Rom. 13.8)

SECOND SUNDAY IN ADVENT, 6 DECEMBER 1998

Readings: Isa. 40.1–11; Lk. 21.25–36; Rom. 13.8–14

I

I read recently a review of a book by the novelist Margaret Forster, not this time a novel, but *Precious Lives*, a memoir of two relatives – her father and her sister-in-law – who had recently died. They were very different, in their personalities and their manner of death: one very old, the other dying of an illness; but, 'With the approach of death [they] became less different. Both of them began to take delight in the smallest things: in drinking a cup of coffee in the sun, in sitting looking at the sea'.[1] And the reviewer comments on the lesson this teaches us:

> In our consumer society, we expect life to be composed of an inexhaustible supply of Great Moments, of images derived from advertising or holiday brochures . . . We expect too much. It's only when life is ebbing away that people remember to appreciate what is around them; what is here, now. Maybe we shouldn't wait until we are dying to try and do the same.[2]

---

1 Cressida Connolly in *The Spectator*, 17 October, 1998, p. 41.
2 Cressida Connolly in *The Spectator*, 17 October, 1998, p. 41.

Even if you leave the television off all or most of the time, as I do, there is simply no escape from the modern world, with the pressures so well evinced by that review – the pressure to snatch at life, to wring from it relentless enjoyment. Just as according to the psalmist you cannot escape God by going to the uttermost parts of the earth, so it is with our world. Consumerism, especially evident at this time of the year, is its way of life. Napoleon and Hitler may both have failed in storming the gates of Moscow, but not McDonald's. That is to state the obvious: we all know very well what our world is like. Far more interesting is the point about the effect of the imminence of death, for, like the eve of execution, it helps to concentrate the mind. Those two dying people had learned what life is about, so that a cup of coffee was as important to them as some once-in-a-lifetime experience.

II

And so to the passage from Romans. Paul is writing to a people just like us, a people who had to obey the law and pay their taxes in a world like ours – a world for the most part pagan and ignorant of the things that truly make for life and make for death. At this stage of the letter, he has moved from exposition of the Gospel to saying something in more detail about what it meant for their daily life. Among other things, what they have to do is to obey God's law, especially as it is set out in the Ten Commandments, summed up as they are in the command that we must love our neighbour. That is the obvious bit. We all know, indeed, perhaps that is the one thing those ignorant of most of the faith know, that we are expected to love our neighbour. But what does it mean, and whence comes the obligation to do so? *Why* should we love our neighbour, rather than competing with him in the rush for worldly gain and success?

The reason lies in that odd and difficult verse on which I once preached a sermon here. 'The hour has now come for you to wake up from slumber, because our salvation is nearer now than when we first believed.' Although perhaps we do not often think about it – and certainly not as often as we ought – the Christian life is lived under the pressure of the end of all things. Whatever else that strange prophecy recorded in Luke means, it means that. 'Be careful, or your hearts will be weighed down with dissipation . . . and the anxieties of life, and that day will close upon you unexpectedly, like a trap.' Whatever is and will be the case about the year 2000, the real millennium, the return of the Lord in glory, the end of all things, is, for us, always imminent.

And that is the motive not for fear or paralysis, not for saying that nothing matters any more, but the reverse. The shorter the time, the more seriously we should take our ordinary day-to-day obligations. A short time ago, a close friend of one of our secretaries, a young man in his twenties, I think, was, to her great distress, killed in a climbing accident. It turned out that the week before, almost as if he had had a premonition of the end, he had made things up with some of his family from whom he had been estranged. And that, I think, is the point here. 'Let no debt remain outstanding, except the continuing debt to love one another.'

One of the things many people do when they know that they are dying – and the mystery in this case is that this man did seem to know – is to put their affairs in order. And that is what Paul is suggesting, in this rather unusual way. Clear your debts – except this one, which can never be cleared.

And the point is this. You have been loved with a great love, the love celebrated earlier in this great letter. 'Christ died for the ungodly . . . God demonstrates his own love for us in this: While we were still sinners, Christ died for us.' While we were still his enemies, God sent his Son, in our place, to break down our estrangement from him. And so the consummation of that great love, the coming of the time when God will wipe away every tear from our eyes, is for us always around the corner, the sun about to rise gloriously after a dark night of sleepless suffering. The expectation of the return of one who has done so much for us can only be promise, not threat. He who has come will come – will return to this dark and wicked world, a light in its darkness, scattering its gloom and unbelief and completing that which was begun in his first coming.

And the message is get on with your daily life, pay your taxes and do your Christmas shopping yet don't make them the ultimate. Only one thing is finally important, 'Let no debt remain outstanding, except the continuing debt to love one another'. It is quite simple: because we have been loved, and loved to the uttermost, the only important obligation is that of love. Do not be encumbered with anything else. Like someone about to die, clear your debts, make peace – and retain only this one. As one recent writer has put it, 'Advent celebrates the dissolution of all obligations in face of this one great obligation, the love which God commands us for himself and for our fellow human beings, both presented to us in the face of Christ'.[3]

III

I began with an illustration of the way in which the imminence of death changed the perspectives of those two people on the world. Of course, the imminence of the end affects people in different ways. In the highly charged atmosphere of my youth, with America and Russia facing each other over a chasm of fear and threat, there was, as you may remember, a song, which went more or less, 'don't you know, my friend, we're on the eve of destruction', and I still remember the article in the student newspaper which speculated about what people would do if they knew that the bomb was about to fall.

---

3   Oliver O'Donovan, *The Desire of the Nations: Rediscovering the Roots of Political Theology* (Cambridge: Cambridge University Press, 1996), p. 253. In the sermon it is recorded slightly wrongly; where Colin has written 'presented to us', the original had 'represented to us'.

Death and Modernity

It is, and remains, the case that we are on the eve not of destruction but of salvation. There was, in Thursday's paper, the story of the schoolboy who, having calculated the odds in favour of and against life, had, apparently calmly, committed suicide. The headline in the paper spoke of his 'flawed logic'. But, of course, it was not the logic that was flawed, but, if I may so put it, his theology. On a mere mathematical calculus, it is little more than a toss-up. It is only the Advent hope, the imminence of salvation, that makes a real difference.

Let me put it another way. We live in an anxious, noisy, greedy world that is inescapable. We earn our livings in it, we consume its goods, drive its cars, fly in its aircraft, add to its pollution and so on. But a bit like those two dying people, we live in expectation and, indeed, enjoyment of something else, something quite different that affects us, or has the power to affect us, as the approach of death affected those two dying people: to appreciate something of the value of things and to enjoy things rightly *because* – not despite the fact that – we know that they are doomed to pass away.

The key is found in our text, which I shall repeat. 'Let no debt remain outstanding, except the continuing debt to love one another.' Our text is, of course, not about our enjoyment of the world, as was that review with which I began, but about our obligations, under God's law, to our fellow Christians first and fellow human beings second. But the way we live in our world – and, remember, it is God's good world, given to us to enjoy – is bound up with this. Paul draws similar lessons to this in his earlier First Letter to the Corinthians, in an apparently odd piece of advice that we should live as though we are not as we are: 'those who mourn as if they did not; those who are happy, as if they were not . . . those who use the things of this world, as if not engrossed in them. For the world in its present form is passing away' (1 Cor. 7.30–31). 'Those who use the things of this world, as if not engrossed in them.' Because for us things are changed, because he has come, has died and risen, will come again – because of that, we can learn to live in the world as God's good gift. We can have our social committees, our hobbies, the things that give us recreation and relief – but don't give them ultimate authority over our lives. There is a way to live even in our noisy consumer society without succumbing to its idolatries – and that is the practice of God's people. 'The night is nearly over; the day is almost here.' Because, in the words of the hymn, we are already children of the day, God will give us the grace to live in our world as his people. Thanks be to him, through Jesus Christ, to whom be glory for ever. Amen.

18

Death and Readiness

> Teach us to number our days aright, that we may gain a heart of wisdom.
>
> (Ps. 90.12)

FUNERAL OF HUGH FRASER, 20 SEPTEMBER 1998

Readings: Ps. 46.1–7, Ps. 90.1–12, Phil. 1.15–26

I

Many here may remember the funeral of Jean Rolls that took place several years ago. I vividly remember the theme of Malcolm Hamblett's[1] sermon, because, perhaps wrongly, it rather shocked me. Its theme was that you never know when death will strike, so be on your guard. Here was a lady, apparently in good health, in her fifties, which is by today's standards – and particularly Hugh's – rather young; and she was swept away. That represents one side of the message of the psalm we have just heard, an apparently rather unrelieved pessimism. 'You turn men back to dust, saying, "Return to dust, O sons of men".' 'You sweep men away in the sleep of death; they are like the new grass of the morning – though in the morning it springs up new, by evening it is dry and withered.'

The message becomes bleaker as the poem continues. Much of the cause of the problem is, according to our writer, human sin. We make our beds and, apparently, have to lie on them. 'All our days pass under your wrath; we finish our years with a moan.' The traditional doctrine of original sin has come in for

---

1 The then minister of Brentwood URC.

some criticism in recent years, and for good reason, in view of the way it has sometimes been formulated. But we cannot escape its truth. For whatever cause, we live in a wicked and violent world and are bound up in a human race which, apparently, is set on self-destruction. That is the reason why our lives are not just finite – limited to between one day and 100-plus years – but often burdened with the kind of troubles which make them in so many ways a trial, make each day a struggle – sometimes with age or illness, sometimes with people, sometimes with the relentless pressures of work in the modern world.

II

That is one side of our life, what one philosopher called its relentless movement, its thrownness towards death. Let me put another. Over twenty years ago, we had an extension built to our house. The builder employed to dig the foundation was an old man[2] whose skill was to be able to dig a beautiful, clean, narrow trench which would need the minimum of concrete. (Unfortunately, it was a summer rather like this one, and I remember sitting one dark evening hearing the rain lashing down and the sides of the trench falling in; our psalmist would have appreciated that, too.) This old man liked to expatiate on the ills of life, particularly old age. But, he said, 'We go on. Life is sweet.' Life is sweet. Whatever else we have to say about this subject, we remember that life is the good gift of God. It is indeed utterly mysterious; who can even define life – have you ever tried it? – let alone understand it. The great thing about the psalms, with their capacity to run the gamut of the emotions from venomous hatred of the persecutor to exultant love of God, is that they present life in all its variety and richness. It happens to be the case that our psalm is one that reflects on the down side, on the evanescence of life and God's judgement on our foolish iniquity.

---

2 Known as 'Wally', the old man is also mentioned in the following sermon, preached on 3 June 2001.

Death and Readiness

But not only that. In no one psalm is gloom the final word. Somehow, their laments are always enclosed in a faith in God's covenant mercies and goodness. It begins with an affirmation of faith: 'Lord, you have been our dwelling place throughout all generations'. And, after many verses of the kind we have heard, pauses with this thought, and our text for today: Psalm 90.12, 'Teach us to number our days aright, that we may gain a heart of wisdom'. He knows that left to ourselves we have no hope of gaining a right perspective on life. If we judge for ourselves, all will look gloomy, or we may force ourselves to believe the opposite, by evading the thought of suffering and death while we can. The crucial words in this verse are 'heart' and 'wisdom'. 'Teach us to number our days aright, that we may gain a heart of wisdom.' First, the heart. We tend to think of the mind as the most important part of us, and the heart something that must be preserved by exercise and eating the right things (though I was pleased to read in the paper the other day that the connection between what we eat and heart disease has been queried in a large survey). For the Hebrews, it was a metaphor for what we really are. 'The Lord looks on the heart', not just on our minds, but what makes us persons: thought, emotion, feelings, the lot. We speak of people being big- or warm-hearted, referring to their whole persons, not their minds alone. And the key to the heart is wisdom. (It is a pity that the translation we heard put it like this, 'that our minds may learn wisdom', instead of a heart of wisdom.)

Wisdom is a remarkably underused word nowadays. I looked it up recently in a dictionary of philosophy and found that it did not even have an entry to itself! In view of the fact that philosophy means the love of wisdom, it shows how far our culture has sunk. We have lost wisdom for mere knowledge, even worse for mere information, as T. S. Eliot lamented even before the so-called information revolution. Wisdom means a capacity to bring together in our living in the world all the things that make for life rather than death: our relation to God, our accumulated experience of people and the world – it is not something that the very young can achieve, or not usually, though as we know, God can achieve wisdom out of all kinds of sources. The old can be foolish and the young wise. But, in general, we have to learn wisdom as the result of the hard lessons of life, and that takes time. And not only that: if we are to read those lessons aright, we must receive our wisdom from God. 'Teach us to number our days aright, that we may gain a heart of wisdom.'

Now, the heart of wisdom consists in 'numbering our days'. What does that mean? I recently heard an Anglican bishop, one for whom I have much respect, say that the job of the church is to teach people how to pray and how to die. I think that is not quite right. My first thought on hearing it was, how negative. Are we not in the church to learn how to live? Of course we are, and to suggest, as is still often suggested, that the Gospel is about training for the next life only is a grievous mistake. Yet there is much in what he says, and I suspect that we do today neglect our responsibility of teaching people how to die. Nevertheless, the balance is put much better in that great evening hymn:

> Teach me to live, that I may dread
> the grave as little as my bed;
> teach me to die, that so I may
> rise glorious at the aweful day.[3]

I think that that is what 'numbering our days' means.

The same translation to which I've already taken exception puts the first line of our text, 'make us know how few are our days'. That is a gilding of the lily, and overinterpretation. The psalmist is indeed concerned with the limits of our life. But numbering our days has a positive side, too. To number our days means also to know that however long or short they are, God has given us something to make of them. I was interested

---

3 *Rejoice and Sing*, 416.

to see in Hugh Fraser's reminiscences how until very recently he attended in London the meetings of the Electoral Reform Society; before that, his life was an astonishing series of calls and responses, of many kinds. He did according to his years, what he believed it was right and possible for him to do. Right *and* possible. We have been given tasks to do, tasks that will present themselves to us during our life. We are too anxious to bring in the kingdom overnight, too anxious to think that if we don't do a thing, it will not get done. I recently wrote to an American academic asking him to write a contribution to a book in honour of a teacher of mine. He replied, 'I'm saying no to everything, but can't say no to this'. Being over-committed, he is having to limit things, but being presented with something he knows is right, he takes it on. That, I think, is a concrete example of what it means to number our days. It means exercising judgement; that is precisely the point of asking God to give us a heart of wisdom.

The balance was put in a similar way by Paul. He knew the weariness of the flesh, the tiredness that comes when the limits are reached. 'I am pulled two ways; my own desire is to depart and be with Christ – that is better by far; but for your sake the greater need is for me to remain in the body.' 'For to me life is Christ, and death is gain.' In that sense, we can have our cake and eat it, though in that sense alone.

III

One thing that numbering our days does not mean is counting, calculating. Of course, we have to plan. There is a warning from Jesus about those who fail to count the cost; they are left with half-built houses. But that is not the same as trying to get things tied up in every detail. Remember the man who built barns in which to store his ever greater wealth. 'You fool, this night your soul is required of you.' Wisdom lies in knowing the measure of things, and it is very hard to achieve. The even greater wisdom lies in trusting the outcome of whatever we do to God. Whether our lives be long or short, we are given something to do with them. When our grandchild died, a message sent by that same one of my teachers I have already mentioned put the positive side: God's creation is very various. In his mysterious goodness, he gives to some of us brief, some long lives, and some something in between. For the psalmist, seventy years was the most that could be expected. For most of us now, it's something between what Hugh and Benjamin,[4] at either end of a century, were given.

And there is one more thing to say. At the table of the Lord, we celebrate the life of one whose life was cut short for us, in the flower of his manhood. He was broken, after a life already given up for others, that we might be whole. We number our days aright if we look to him, who for the joy that was set before him, endured the cross, despising the shame, and is set at the right hand of God.

---

4   Colin Gunton's grandson, Benjamin Gunton.

19

Life and the Spirit

Then the angel showed me the river of the water of life, as clear as crystal, flowing from the throne of God and of the Lamb down the middle of the great street of the city.

(Rev. 22.1–2a)

PENTECOST SUNDAY, 3 JUNE 2001

Readings: Ezek. 47.1–12; Rev. 22.1–7; Jn 7.37–44

I

Years ago, when we had an extension built on the back of our house, the builder employed an old man to dig the foundations.[1] He was used because of the meticulous character of his digging, keeping the trench narrow and the cost of the concrete down. He was a melancholy man, very aware of the ills of ageing and dying, but I remember him saying, 'Life is sweet'. Life is something we all recognize, but can almost certainly not define it (try it). It is one of those mysteries of our world which is so central to everything, that it is impossible to describe it in terms of other things. It is unique, mysterious and an ultimate value. And it is the gift of God through his Holy Spirit, whom the creed describes as, 'The Lord and giver of life'. 'And in the Holy Spirit, the Lord and Giver of Life.'

That is the credal confession for today, and it follows naturally after last month's treatment of the resurrection which, as we shall see, is the key to the matter. And, having begun with the theme of life, let me introduce another, which is also

---

1 Also mentioned in the funeral sermon preached on 20 September 1998.

important for our theme of God the Holy Spirit. In the fourth century, there lived a bishop and theologian, Basil of Caesarea. We shall meet him also in the next sermon, a fortnight hence. According to him, the Holy Spirit is the one who perfects the work of God the Father. God's work begins with the Father, goes through the Son and reaches its completion in the Spirit. Wherever anything in the world goes right, we might say, God does it through his Spirit. Wherever, anywhere in the world, there is goodness, truth or beauty, there we see the work of the Spirit of the Father.

And to bring the two themes together: central among the Spirit's gifts is the gift of life. That is the aspect of his work that the creed concentrates on, and for very good reasons. If there is one theme that dominates the Scriptures, from the beginning to the end, it is life. Life is the Spirit's greatest gift, and in some ways it is the central theme of all Scripture. I looked again in preparation for this sermon at the central verses of the account of creation in Genesis 1, and might have used it for the Old Testament reading had not the Ezekiel passage, to which we shall come, seemed more appropriate to go with the verses from John which we heard. Both of them are concerned with teeming life, with God's finest gift in all its abundance.

But, as we know too well these days, there is also death; death which takes away those we love and which seems to destroy relationships, achievements, everything. While there is indeed life, there is also death. In that light, let us explore some things the Bible has to say about the Spirit.

II

Scripture is often oblique in its references to the Spirit. That is because the Spirit is the most elusive of the three persons of the Trinity. There is a reason for this. According to John's Gospel, Jesus comes so that we may know God the Father. To be a Christian is to know Jesus and, through him, the Father.

Life and the Spirit

We don't know the Spirit in the same way, for we know *through* him. And the elusiveness supplies the reason for the way in which the Spirit is described: like fire or wind in the story we know best, but also in our readings in terms of water. That takes us straight back to what I said at the beginning about life. Water is the source of life, for Scripture as it is for modern science. And the Spirit is like water, like water on the thirsty ground is the life-giving power of God.

Towards the end of the book of Ezekiel, we read the prophet's vision of water flowing from under the podium of the temple, the place where God's presence is to be found. It begins as a trickle and, as it flows eastwards, it becomes a mighty river. Its destination is the desert around the Dead Sea, where nothing will grow. 'There will be large numbers of fish, because this water flows there and makes the water fresh; so where the river flows, everything will live.' Where the Spirit is, there will be life.

In our reading from John's Gospel, we see something of the greatest of all the Spirit's gifts, the fact that he turns us to Jesus. In Isaiah 55, 'Come, all you who are thirsty, come to the waters'. John's Gospel takes up that theme, as he takes up so much from Isaiah. Jesus cries out, 'If anyone is thirsty, let him come to me and drink'. 'By this', explains John, 'he meant the Spirit, whom those who believed in him were later to receive'. So, two visions, likening the Spirit to abundant, life-giving water, poured out by the God and Father of our Lord Jesus Christ.

We can be misled into expecting the wrong things if we think of the Spirit only in terms of the apparent ecstasy of Acts 2. Biblical language of the Spirit is far richer and all-encompassing than this. For example, when Scripture speaks of the power, or energy or glory of God, that is often a reference to the Spirit. We must think of the Spirit not as an isolated force, and certainly not as a warm feeling, but as the power of God the Father in action – what Irenaeus called one of the two hands of God the Father, the Son and the Spirit.

The Spirit is the power of God in action, the power which keeps things going and at the last will make all things new, will, through Jesus Christ, perfect everything to his glory. Such measure of confidence as we have in God – and it is different for all of us – comes from the Spirit through Jesus Christ our Lord. But what does that mean, concretely?

III

All abundance, all life, all good comes from God the Father, the source of all blessings, through his Son and the Spirit who perfects his work.

We can look at this under a number of levels, beginning with the abundant life that we see all around us. We often worry about the devastation brought about by our building over and pollution of the earth, but leave any part of it alone for long and, so long as there is water, rampant life will break out, cracking concrete and covering everything with a carpet of riotous green. God is not a God who leaves his creation to its own devices; through his Spirit he renews it daily, indeed every moment, giving seed for the sower, bread for the hungry. But as we know all too well, that life is also fragile, for all things that come into being also come to an end, as will our world in God's good time. As we have heard, the Spirit gives life, but when he is withdrawn, it is taken away. 'When you take away their breath, they die and return to the dust from which they came.' The Lord the Spirit gives life, but it is a gift, dependent on the giver, and given only for a time.

But there is a second level, embracing this and encompassing it with even greater richness and abundance. If we want to understand the life that the Spirit gives, we must look above all at the resurrection of Jesus. Paul speaks of the Spirit of him who raised from the dead our Lord Jesus Christ (Rom. 8.11) and the promise that he will give us, too, the life of the age to come. The one who raised from the dead our Lord Jesus Christ is indeed the Lord and giver of life. There is the guarantee of our life, too. Because of Jesus, the life that is given and taken away will at the last be replaced, succeeded, by a life that cannot be taken away, a life which we cannot begin to imagine but which waits for those for whom he died. In that imperishable hope we commit those who die to the Lord, and ourselves live our lives.

But, and this is the third feature, this is not simply a future hope. Let us return to our images of water. For Ezekiel, the waters flow from the sanctuary in Jerusalem, from the place where the Lord has made his dwelling to the land round about. For John, that sanctuary is now Jesus Christ, the crucified and risen, where God took up his dwelling through that same Spirit. Because he is risen and ascended to God the Father, the life of the world to come flows into our world wherever he is worshipped and acknowledged. The city of the future, the city which is to come, whose builder and maker is God, comes down among us. That is the promise of the Spirit, that the blessings of the age to come are anticipated in the here and now, that already we can share something of the heavenly banquet in the present.

What does that mean? Several things. 'We believe in life before death', says the famous Christian Aid slogan, and that is right. Feeding the hungry, housing the homeless is part of it, part of the way the abundant life of the Spirit flows beyond the walls of the church to the parched world around. I sometimes wonder, however, whether sometimes the modern church thinks that that is the main thing. If so, it is in danger of losing itself in works, in an activism that loads too much on us, too little on God's saving action. On the other hand, we do not have a merely 'religious' message. I remember the student sermons we used to preach to sermon class, offering the congregation joy, new life and the rest. Well, there is that, too, but we must not be unrealistic, and must certainly not suggest that to be a Christian is to live in a continual haze of well-being. The Spirit is not a warm feeling, but the Lord and giver of life. Jesus himself, the one led by the Spirit, did not sail through life untroubled, nor should we expect to. Life is a blessed gift, but also a struggle. In the midst of life, we are in death.

And that is the key to the matter. We do not struggle alone. The life of the age to come, the water that flows from the side of Jesus, the abundant teeming life of the Spirit, comes to us in all kinds of ways, and especially, where Jesus is acknowledged and lived. One friend of mine likes to say that the Spirit is to be found as much in routine as in the ecstatic and special, and he is right. Above all, we must not forget the most important routine of all, our weekly worship, where Jesus is set forth. From him flows everything else and, especially, the mutual support and love that keeps us going in the life of the people of God – the tears that we are sometimes able to share and to wipe away. If we look through Jesus to the ordinary, and especially the ordinary things of our life together, we shall find the Spirit. For there is a sense in which Jesus is ordinary, the Son of God become human for us, and, because God raised him from the dead, our everyday lives can become the place now where his love is received and lived out, in all the joys and sorrows of our existence. 'Where the water flows, everything will live.'

20

The Trinity and Worship

> When the advocate has come, whom I shall send you from the Father – the Spirit of truth who issues from the Father – he will bear witness to me.
>
> (Jn 15.26)

17 JUNE 2001

Readings: Ezek. 36.22–8; Rev. 1.9–16; Jn 14.15–26

I

It was reported recently that the television gardener Alan Titchmarsh does not like being famous. Who wants to be recognized everywhere? Anonymity, he says, is a blessing. And it is true that once you have any kind of public face, people are likely to take up what you say or what you do and be critical about it. It even happens sometimes to those who lead worship. It happened to Basil, Bishop of Caesarea in the fourth century. Some of his congregation took exception to the fact that he seemed to be using contradictory forms of words about God when he was leading worship. Sometimes he said, 'Glory to the Father through the Son and in the Spirit'; and sometimes, 'Glory to the Father with the Son together with the Holy Spirit'. Behind this lies a quite simple question. When we worship, do we worship God the Father through the Son and in the Spirit, or do we worship all three together?

The first of the two forms is extremely important and takes us to the very heart of Christian worship. To worship God the Father through the Son and in the Spirit reminds us that our worship is not an ordinary activity, something that we simply decide to do like taking up painting or watching cricket. It is, first of all, something God does in, with and for us. Worship is the gift of God the Spirit, who, through his Son, enables us to come before the Father's throne as his people. That is why we hear, or should hear, words of Scripture at the beginning of our worship, speaking a word from beyond us that calls us into God's presence. Worship is a gift: we come to the Father through the Son and in the Spirit because they enable us to do what otherwise would be impossible for sinful human beings. To put it another way, worship is made possible and real by the fact that Jesus rose from the dead and sits at the right hand of the Father.

Yet the church in its wisdom decided that the second formula was necessary too. Two weeks ago, the article of the creed which we examined concerned the Holy Spirit as the Lord and Giver of Life. Today we come to another feature of the confession of the Spirit: 'the Holy Spirit . . . who is worshipped and glorified together with the Father and the Son'. What are we to make of that? Well, a sermon is not a theological lecture, and the way to approach our topic is through Scripture, so let us examine a text from the book which most carefully expresses a theology of the Holy Spirit, the Gospel of John.

II

'When the advocate has come, whom I shall send you from the Father – the Spirit of truth who issues from the Father – he will bear witness to me.' There are so many things that can be said of this text, and it would become so complicated, that I shall list a number of points which together will, I hope, show something of what this very profound writer is telling us.

First, Jesus speaks about the Holy Spirit in terms of one who will come to his disciples when his bodily presence is taken away, when he dies, rises and ascends to the right hand of the Father. Of course, we know that John is writing after the event. He is almost certainly, as a matter of fact, putting into the mouth of Jesus things learned with the benefit of hindsight.

The Trinity and Worship

John's Gospel gains its unique character from the fact that it is a meditation on the meaning of Jesus from the point of view of the church's experiences of living the Gospel. It need not trouble us if Jesus did not speak quite precisely these words, for what matters is the truth that we learn about the way God is and is with and for us. And the simple point is this. Historically, in the first century AD, God came to be with us in Jesus; once Jesus is no longer present in the same way, the Spirit is the one by whom his presence continues to be made real.

Second, the Spirit is described as the 'advocate'. There have been various translations for the Greek *paracletos*, which John uses to describe the kind of being that the Spirit is and the kind of things that he does. The traditional translation is 'comforter', meaning one who gives strength, not comfort in the modern sense; now the translators prefer 'counsellor' or 'advocate'. I once heard in a sermon the activity of the Spirit explained as being like that of supporters at a football match, literally, one who calls alongside. The word combines the notions of advocacy, support, strengthening.

Third, there is more, for our text also describes the paraclete as the Spirit of truth. For John, 'truth' means Jesus, who is God's truth and faithfulness in action: 'the way, the truth and the life'. So we have the Spirit who is our advocate and supporter, but only so as he is bound up with Jesus, who is the truth. Already our text is taking a threefold shape, and this comes out in other words that it contains: 'whom I shall send you from the Father – the Spirit of truth who issues from the Father'. That encapsulates a vast range of points, but let me be as simple and straightforward as possible. The Spirit is God's free and transcendent power operating in and towards his world, one of the two hands by which God gets things done. 'By the word of the Lord the heavens were made, their starry host by the breath of his mouth' (Ps. 33.6). The Spirit is the Father's way of giving life, of warming hearts, as we heard in the Ezekiel reading, of making the world as it should be. And he comes to the world through Jesus. Because Jesus is the truth of God in action, because he died for the sins of the world and was raised, because of what he was and is and does, he has become the channel for that power, the Spirit of God active and at work in the world.

And that takes me to a fourth, and also important, point. The theme around which this sermon is being organized is worship, and we need to refer to one other text from our Gospel to develop our examination of what John is saying. Jesus is the truth, as we have seen, and the Spirit of truth is the Spirit of Jesus Christ. Those who worship the Father must do so, says Jesus elsewhere in this Gospel, in spirit and in truth (Jn 4.24). And that means precisely what our text tells us: through the Spirit and Jesus. We have what can be called a descending and ascending movement: the Spirit comes from the Father, through Jesus, so that we can ascend to God the Father, also through him. There you have Christian worship in a nutshell.

But, and this is the fifth and final point, it is obvious from all of this that you don't have to choose between Basil's two forms of blessing. We do indeed come to the Father through Jesus and in the Spirit. But they are at the same time the ones who do God's work in the world, becoming man, living, dying and rising, on the one hand; and, on the other, making that risen and ascended saviour present to us week by week and day by day. Let me return to that simple analogy of the Son and the Spirit as the two hands of God the Father. Our hands are ourselves in action. We use them to greet, to bless and, sometimes, to injure, and what they do, we do. That is the way to understand what John is telling us. Christ and the Spirit do God's work as God, for only God can do the things that they do, only God can bring sinful and wicked man cleansed to the holy Father, only God can warm the hearts of those hardened in sin so that they are able and willing to praise the one who made them. And so we praise and worship those by whom we are enabled to worship, one God, made known in three persons.

This is the season of Trinity, and it reminds us that Christians do not worship any old God, but a very particular one, the one made known through Jesus Christ. Earlier in the sermon I said that worship is possible for two reasons: because Jesus is risen and at the right hand of the Father and because God sends his Spirit so that we may worship him. Not only do we worship in this way, but the very nature of our worship makes us realize that the ones through whom we worship belong with God the Father in the communion that is the one God. You cannot have any one without the other two, and so we worship one God, as we say, in three persons. We thus worship all three together, simply because the three are one God. This is not abstruse theology, but a simple account of how things happen, and who our God is.

III

Why is all this important? Let me try to reflect on that which I have already made much of, our worship. We are all beings who worship something, whatever is most important for us, which gives value to our lives. That is part of what it is to be human. Man was not made for freedom, said Luther, he must be the slave of either God or the Devil. Similarly, Paul Tillich used to say that everyone has what he called an ultimate concern, that which makes him or her tick. There is something at the centre of all our lives, and we only have to watch the occasional television advertisement to see what we are in our world encouraged to make the centre of our lives and values. Yet, to worship anything but the one true God is idolatry and destroys us, because to worship anything that is not God is to worship that which is not worthy of worship and will turn on us and rend us. Those who worship power, for example, as the great tyrants have done and continue to do, are the ones who bring war and destruction, and one could go on.

Idolatry is the worship of the lie, that which claims to be the source of life but cannot be. We all succumb to it, all without exception. Day after day, I fall into the temptation of putting my trust in the things of this world: money, success, pleasure, security. The only cure for our lost condition is the one who is the truth made man, Jesus Christ our Lord. And the only one who can hold us to him is God the Holy Spirit, 'the Spirit of truth who issues from the Father'. Without those two hands we remain lost souls, wandering the earth in search of something that can satisfy.

But the truth of the Gospel is that we are not lost, for we live under the promise that our idolatries, petty and great, are not the final truth to be told about ourselves. We truly come to the Father through Christ and the Spirit. We must say, therefore, that worship has a redemptive function, for we need to be turned away from ourselves and our sins to the holy God who is our creator and our only truth. We are only truly ourselves when we turn away from ourselves in worship. But that is less important than an even greater truth, for true worship is worship of God for his own sake, for his own glory and beauty. That, I think, is the reason for the austerity of Ezekiel's picture of God, a God who does things for the sake of his name, his glory, his holiness, and nothing else. This reflects something that is also an everyday truth. The good things of life, the beauty of nature and of art, the love of those who care for us, do indeed enhance our lives. Yet they are of value not first of all because of that, but because of what they are in themselves. A great painting or a perfect rose are valuable in themselves, for what they are. That is even more true of human beings, who are to be loved and cherished for themselves before they are valued for what they give to us. How much more true is that of our God. We worship God both because he is worshipful in his eternal and holy love and glory, but also because we are beings who are made to worship and are only truly ourselves as we worship the triune God, the God who lives for ever in the beauty of holiness. And so with Basil we can say both, 'Glory to the Father through the Son and in the Spirit'; and 'Glory to the Father with the Son together with the Holy Spirit' – as it was in the beginning, is now, and ever shall be, world without end, Amen.

21

The Meaning of Love

> So Jacob served seven years for Rachel, and they seemed to him but a few days because of the love he had for her.
>
> (Gen. 29.20)

MARRIAGE OF NINA FRASER AND JONATHAN RODD,
23 SEPTEMBER 2000

Readings: Gen. 29.10–28; 1 Cor. 13.1–13

It is one of the less attractive features of our mass culture that, often for reasons of gain, the currency of our language becomes debased, and words which once contributed to our life together in society now look set to endanger it. Contrast, for example, the meaning Paul gives to the word at the centre of the reading you have chosen, and the use made of it in so much popular 'culture'. 'Love' has always carried a vast range of meanings – C. S. Lewis wrote in a well-known book of *The Four Loves* – but today I think that we are not always clear about the deeper meaning contained in your passage. I shall speak of that later, but want to begin not with that, but with what, for my money, is one of the greatest celebrations of romantic love in literature.

'So Jacob served seven years for Rachel, and they seemed to him but a few days because of the love he had for her' (Gen. 29.20). What an astonishing few words; ponder them for a moment. Things, of course, were not always like that, and the eventual marriage of Jacob and Rachel experienced much the same mixture of joy and grief, comedy and tragedy, errors and repentance, that are to be experienced in any human pairing. If we consider the story as a whole, we shall see that the Bible is both romantic and realistic in its treatment of relations between the sexes. Could there be anything more romantic than that wonderful text? Or anything more realistic than the fact that Jacob was where he was because his mother had led him to deceive his aged father and cheat his brother out of his birthright? The leader of a group studying the Bible somewhere told me recently how uncomfortable many of his charges were about the Old Testament, how relieved when they reached the apparently calmer waters of the New. But where would we be without that verse? And, in any case, that set of books is, in its own way, as realistic about the human condition as is the writer of the tangled story of Abraham and Isaac, Jacob, Leah and Rachel.

The reading from 1 Corinthians is one of the most moving and poetic chapters in Scripture, and even the worst efforts of modern translators cannot take away its poetry. Like the best poetry, however, it is utterly realistic, as we shall see if we look at it in its context and, particularly, if we read a little between its lines. It is realistic, first of all, in its barbed undertones. Paul is writing to a quarrelsome and disunited community. When he says such things as 'love is not jealous or boastful; it is not arrogant or rude', the suggestion is that all these things *do* characterize the behaviour of those to whom he is writing. The chapter is a rebuke as well as a celebration of the glories of the love of which Paul is speaking, and we ignore at our peril the capacity of this passage to reveal our failures and point us to the place of their healing.

And that takes me to the second aspect of the passage's realism about love. It is realistic in that it shows that life needs an – I suppose you could say *emotional* – depth that goes deeper than even the best actions. 'If I give my body to be burned, but have not love, I gain nothing.' If, like that grumpily gentlemanly writer, W. S. Gilbert, I die saving a lady from drowning, and yet do it without *heart* . . . The heart is the key, because it is that which makes us tick in more ways than one. When I have offended, it is often not because I have done that which I ought not to have done, or failed to do that which I ought, but rather because of the manner in which I have acted or failed to act. It is, I suppose, a matter of the tone of our lives. And the important point here is that just as musical tones can be developed and enhanced, so can the heart be trained. In one of her philosophy books, Iris Murdoch develops a parable of a woman who finds it hard to like her daughter-in-law because she finds her rather loud and vulgar. She comes to like her by directing to her an attitude of loving attention, enabling herself to see that she is not loud, but lively. Love may come from the heart, but it can also be learned, indeed has to be, for marriage is, among other things, a training in love, for example, learning to find loveable some things in the other that might otherwise be irritating. (Not to expect things to come too easily is perhaps one of the keys to married love, while false expectations are perhaps in our day one of the causes of unnecessary failure.)

All this is very hard, indeed impossible, to achieve as we are and on our own, even as the most united and loving couple. That is why we need to give the closest attention to the third feature of this chapter. The chapter 1 Corinthians 13 draws its pattern from a life – and a death – to whose proclamation Paul gave his all. The central passage of the chapter, from which I have already quoted, could be a description of the bearing and the life of Jesus, and there is little doubt that that is how Paul intended it. 'Love bears all things, believes all things, hopes all things, endures all things.' As a description of what is expected of us, that might be a terrible burden. But as a description of what this man did and was, it is the source only of encouragement.

Let us follow up a little of why this might be so. The love of which Paul is speaking in this passage is not something abstract, not an ideal, not a theory, but a person. 'God is love', says the much-quoted text, but it is not any old love, but love of a particular kind. It is love in action, a love which lived and died a particular human life, but a human life which was also at the same time the love of God *happening* among us, in person. And it happened among us not because we deserved it — in fact, the very opposite — but because we needed it. 'Love to the loveless shown, that they might lovely be',[1] go the words of the old hymn, and that says it all.

We don't find it easy to be lovely, especially sometimes, I regret to say, to those closest to us. It was reported the other day that two of the members of the *Ground Force* team[2] quarrelled so much that someone thought they must be married. A sour reflection, perhaps, and one you might not think appropriate for a day like this. But it enables us to learn that there is a need for the heart not only to be trained, to grow deeper into the love without which we are not as fully human as we might be, but also to receive love from the one who is its source. The one who 'bears all things, believes all things, hopes all things, endures all things' for us, brought and brings us the love of God — is the love of God in action — in order that during the whole of life's long process from birth to death we might learn to love, might have our hearts trained in love in what the cliché calls the crucible of our experience.

Of all the places in which that training takes place, marriage is at once the most difficult and the most rewarding. It is the most difficult because it calls on powers that we often do not have though, as we have seen, they are available to us in the love of God made man for us. But it is the most rewarding, because in the faithful love of man and woman, with its slow movement from early passion to settled age, is to be found the greatest reflection of that love for the other which Jesus showed and was. Without it, all the other loves fall apart or become stunted. All others depend on this, because unless love is learned here, it is unlikely to flourish elsewhere. Coleridge said, rather quaintly, as it now seems to us, that personal affections expand 'like the circles of a Lake — the Love of our

---

1 *Rejoice and Sing*, 207
2 A television gardening programme.

The Meaning of Love

Friends, parents and neighbours leads us to the love of Country to the love of all Mankind. The intensity of private attachment encourages, not prevents, universal philanthropy'. What begins in a private love spreads its reality and its message out into the world about it.

And so to end where I began, with the fate of that word 'love'. The life and death, and especially the resurrection, of the one who was God's love in action shows that the corruption of our language and life is not the final thing to say about our world. While he is at the centre, even that word can be redeemed. Real love is to be found in the one who was and is and will be God's love poured out into our world. That is the rock that founds our human love and will support your marriage as you set out on the greatest of life's journeys of discovery. 'Love bears all things, believes all things, hopes all things, endures all things': live in that hope and that promise, and you will not go far wrong.

22

The Resurrection and the Ascension

Do not hold onto me, for I have not yet returned to the Father.
(Jn 20.17)

EASTER SUNDAY, 20 APRIL 2003

Readings: Ps. 118; Jn 20.1–18; Acts 10.34–43

I

When I was a child, I tended to worry a little about the dating of the resurrection. Does it not say that Jesus would rise 'after three days'? But it always seemed to me to be after two. The writers of the creed, we might observe, noted the discrepancy, and firmly wrote, 'on the third day he rose again', because that is more accurate. We do not, of course, need to worry. Just as forty days, or forty years, is a Hebraism for 'a long time', so 'three days' is a way of saying, 'a short time'. In this case, long enough that we can be sure that Jesus was really dead, not just revived after a swoon, as is sometimes claimed by the sceptics. There is another mathematical worry, too. Did the ascension happen soon after the resurrection, as John's Gospel seems to suggest, or was it after forty days, as in Acts? Again, it is the meaning and not the mathematics with which we are concerned. I remember long ago preaching on the text, 'and the number of the beast was 666', and stressing the slogan that mathematics may be magic, but wisdom is better. So it is here, for John – or perhaps Luke in Acts – plays around with the chronology of the story of Jesus' last days on earth in order to make a specific point. Luke uses the forty-day period to link the end of Jesus' story with other forties in Scripture. John has another theological end in view. For him, the ascension happens not only more quickly, but almost without our being able to notice it. In our story, the risen Christ appears only to be around in his immediately risen form for a very short time. Let us follow parts of the story through to see why this might be.

II

The miracle of the resurrection is brought out in two ways: the discovery of the empty tomb and the almost embarrassing story of mistaken identity. John's account, like that of all the other Gospels except Luke's, makes Mary Magdalene the first witness of the empty tomb, and she reappears in the second half of the reading that we heard. The story is well known. Mary has just told the angels guarding the empty tomb that someone has taken Jesus' body away and turns and sees not a dead body but a living man behind her. Remember the rhetorical question the angel asks in Luke's account, 'Why do you seek the living among the dead?' This is John's way of making the same point. Mary still believes that Jesus is dead. What else is to be expected? Dead men do not rise from the dead; they simply do not. That gives one reason why she does not recognize Jesus. We often see only what we expect to see; really to see what is there requires a process of education. Babies cannot see in the sense that we can when they emerge into the world; what they see was described by William James as a blooming, buzzing confusion, and they have to learn to distinguish first their mother and then other people and things in the world. Similarly, people who draw and paint see the world in some ways more clearly than I do. And if you recently saw a man twisted and dead after being taken down from a place of execution, then you are simply not able to see him – unless you are given eyes.

However, I think that there is also a second reason for Mary's failure. It seems to be a feature of Jesus' appearances

The Resurrection and the Ascension

after the resurrection – and before the ascension – that he is not recognized. Again, Luke has a parallel, saying that the eyes of the couple on the road to Emmaus 'were kept from recognizing' Jesus. Only when he breaks bread do they realize who he is. Here it is not action but speech that does the trick. Mary thinks that this man is the gardener and asks him whether he has moved the body. It is Jesus' calling her by name – as he has called each one of us by name to bring us to this place this morning – which does the trick. 'Jesus said to her, "Mary". She turned to him and cried out in Aramaic, "Rabboni" (which means teacher).' It is one of the great recognition scenes in all literature (and, incidentally, the key to the Bible's understanding of revelation).

But she is forbidden the embrace that would be the natural response to seeing one raised from the dead. In another revelatory scene, perhaps most famously depicted by Titian's painting in the National Gallery, 'Do not hold on to me, for I have not yet returned to the Father' – or, rather, in the simple meaning of the Greek, 'do not touch me' (the recent translations, 'do not cling to me', 'do not hold on to me', over-egg the pudding, making more of the text than is there). The point is simply that Jesus is not yet ready to be touched, because there seems to be something transitional about his condition. Later on, in this same chapter, he is to tell Thomas to put his hands into the wounds he still carries, definitely to touch him. But now, 'do not touch me'. Why? Jesus himself gives the reason, 'for I have not yet ascended to the Father'. This suggests that, for John, the events that are told in the remainder of the Gospel happen after the ascension. From now on, when Jesus appears to the disciples and, later on, to Paul in the account in Acts, there is no doubt who he is, as there will be no doubt when he returns in glory to judge the living and the dead. Here, he is not yet ready for that.

What is John telling us? It is that the ascension, as that which represents the end of Jesus' earthly story, is in some respects more important than the resurrection. The latter is, as I have said, transitional because it is part of Jesus' movement from birth through death to his reign in glory at the right hand of the Father. His concluding words seem to me to make that point. 'I am ascending' – note the present tense, 'I ascend', as if it were happening at that very moment – 'to my Father and your Father, to my God and your God'. There is the point. Notice the link, the repeated 'my and your'. That is why he ascends, to make the link between God and us, to be for ever the ladder between heaven and earth, the way to God the Father. He is not that, simply, as risen, but as risen and ascended.

The lesson for us to learn is that the resurrection is not just a miracle to be used to demonstrate the truth of the Christian faith to unbelievers. It is quite clear, in any case, that nobody 'sees' even this unless he is given eyes to see. The resurrection is, to be sure, a mighty miracle, the miracle of all miracles. But it is the one who is raised that makes all the difference: God's holy one, recently died for the sins of the world on Calvary. The resurrection is the miracle it is because it is the one who gave his life for the whole world who rose, and rose so that we might be able to come to the one who is his Father as our Father.

III

Thus the risen Christ is, as we see him in the garden and as Mary met him, one whose story is 'incomplete'; who is still on the way. And yet the measure of incompleteness, of the Lord still on his way, does not in the least detract from the fact that here something earth-shatteringly new has taken place. It is new, and yet a new thing that happens to the old world. God does not make a new world. His love is for the old world, the old world that he created and yet rejects his love even when it comes in the form of his only Son. The key to that aspect lies in the fact that Mary takes Jesus to be the gardener. Who was the first gardener? Adam. Mary thinks that she is still meeting the old Adam, not the new Adam, who had borne the flesh of Adam, borne it under the conditions of our fall, borne it to the

The Resurrection and the Ascension

last under the judgement of God on the cross. This gardener is the second Adam, the one who went over the human story again, teaching us, as I said in the last sermon, to be human again. The risen Jesus is no longer the man weighted down by the sin and evil of the world but has been set free to the life of the age to come, liberated from the powers of corruption and nothingness to the glorious freedom of the children of God.

This means that although there is a sense in which the risen Jesus, is, so to speak, at this stage of the story in transit, between his birth and his ascension, what has happened is something that has changed the world for ever. There was in last week's *Spectator* an article about Holbein's painting, *Dead Christ in the Tomb*, which you may have seen in the 'Seeing Salvation' exhibition at the National Gallery a few years ago:

> it shows Christ's coffin with one side removed to reveal an emaciated body on a crumpled white shroud. *Rigor mortis* has set in, the hands and feet still claw in their death agony, the mouth and eyes remain open. Muscle tone has begun to collapse and the flesh has taken on the green hue of putrefaction . . .

And the point comes at the end of the article, 'Holbein understood and demonstrated a very simple truth: for a man so utterly dead to come back to life really will require nothing less than a miracle'.[1]

That it happened to this man means that through him the whole of creation dates its renewal from that day:

> For well we know this weary, soiled earth
> is yet thine own by right of its new birth,
> since that great cross on Calvary
> redeemed it from its fault and shame to thee.[2]

---

1 Michael Prodger, 'The Word Made Flesh', *The Spectator*, 19 April 2003, p. 41.
2 *Rejoice and Sing*, 485.

This can be nowhere better encapsulated than in a favourite quotation of mine from G. K. Chesterton:

> On the third day the friends of Christ coming at daybreak to the place found the grave empty and the stone rolled away. In varying ways they realised the new wonder; but even they hardly realised that the world had died in the night. What they were looking at was the first day of a new creation, with a new heaven and a new earth; and in the semblance of the gardener God walked again in the garden, in the cool not of the evening but the dawn.[3]

It is indeed the dawn of a new age, a dawn of the age in which we live because he has now gone to the Father who is our Father. And another point from the article on Holbein as we move to the next stage of our worship. 'The Easter story started with Jesus declaring to his disciples, "This is my body", well, here it is.'

---

3   G. K. Chesterton, *The Everlasting Man* (London: Burnes & Oates, 1974), p. 247.

23

Ascension and the Perfect Sacrifice

> But when this priest had offered for all time one sacrifice for sins, he sat down at the right hand of God.
>
> (Heb. 10.12)

SUNDAY BEFORE ASCENSION, 5 MAY 2002

Readings: Lev. 16.11–24; Heb. 10.11–12; Lk. 24.45–53

I

If you take a boat from Greenwich upriver, you can notice beyond the north bank of the Thames a newish building looking in some ways like a cathedral. It is, of course, a bank. Many banks are cathedral-like buildings. There is one near Bank Station, built by Lutyens, whose entrance hall is marbled and vast, a building holy to the god of money. Banks are like temples in a number of ways: exchange goes on there, and if you get an interview with the manager, you are admitted into the 'inner sanctum', like Aaron into the Holy of Holies. Now, I am introducing the sermon in this way not only to try to make sense of the apparently strange reading from Leviticus, but to suggest something else. We think of the Hebrew Day of Atonement, at least as it is described in Leviticus, as a kind of primitive survival and, in a sense, as our reading from Hebrews suggests, it is. But a far stronger point can be made in its favour. What is going on in the ancient temple is far more real than what goes on in banks.

Now, of course, that has to be qualified. A banker friend of mine once said to me that money nowadays is ultimately unreal, simply the movement of paper and, of course, in the age of the computer, often not even that. I replied, for something that is unreal, it certainly manages to destroy a lot of people. It is real in that sense. But not as real as what is going on in Leviticus. Reality is our relations to God and to one another. That is what really shapes our lives. Reality is being holy before the Lord, being cleansed from the burden of sin that clings so closely, being set free from – among other things – the power of money and other distorting features of our life to shape our lives, to make us what we really are. In that light, let us look at some of the things going on in Leviticus 16.

The chapter is about atonement, being set free from the effects of sin. Often when we have done wrong, or had wrong done to us, we feel unclean, dirtied in some way. There was a young man on the train the other day having an angry and loud row by mobile telephone with someone who, it became clear, was his girlfriend, though for how much longer . . . Every other word, almost, began with an f, and I got off the train generally disgusted. Israel's position in the world was a special one. Called out of the nations, blessed beyond all others, her response of gratitude and praise was to be holy as her God is holy. But as we know in our own lives, things did not go as they ought. Their life was marked, as our text says, by 'uncleanness and rebellion' (Lev. 16.16). And what we read of in this passage is the means, the god-given means, by which they were to be cleansed, each year, and so begin again with what we call a clean – and notice that word again – slate.

It meant that someone had to go before God, the God who is too holy to bear uncleanness, on their behalf, into the fearful and holy place which God had appointed. This was the high priest's calling and responsibility. But to come face to face with God is, so long as he is still imperfect, to die. No one can see God and live, as Scripture repeatedly affirms. And so Aaron first makes an offering for himself in which the blood – or life – of the perfect animal carries off the filth that he has accumulated over the year. Then he is fit to do the same on behalf of the people of Israel. Like soap and water cleansing away a day's labour, the offering, not by magic but because it was the way

Ascension and the Perfect Sacrifice

God had appointed, carried off into the desert the uncleanness of the people. Let us not be mistaken about this. It worked, far better than our ways of trying to cleanse the public realm by fining and putting people into prison. And our New Testament writer, even though he wants to show us something better, agrees that it did, to an extent. The sacrifices, he says, made the people outwardly clean, but could not perfect them. Therefore 'the law [of sacrifice] is but a shadow of the good things to come'. Shadow, but not yet substance; not completely unreal, but not quite the real thing either.

II

What, then, is the real thing? According to our writer, it is Jesus, the one who is like us in all things sin apart. As I heard through the opening chapters of the letter to the Hebrews the other day, I was struck again by the emphatic emphasis the writer makes on this: our brother, the one who is like us, shares our life and, like us, is made holy. One of my colleagues said to me recently that our text contains the two most important words in this book: '*he sat* down at the right hand of God'. Why should that be so? Partly because it represents something finished, complete, the once-and-for-all work on the cross, which has changed things for ever. The reference of 'he sat' is to Jesus' ascension, that rather neglected clause of the creed, and not only because it falls on a Thursday. 'He ascended into heaven' says the creed, and so, clearly, it is judged to be essential to our understanding of our faith. Why?

1

Let me approach the claim of our text indirectly, by speaking first of the ascension in general. It marks in one sense the end, but in another the promise of the end, of a different kind of end, to Jesus' life. In one sense, the end, because it fulfils the point made by Jesus in John's Gospel that he must go away and return to the Father, so that the Spirit may come. He has left the scene. That is why in our celebration of the Lord's Supper we use the words, 'in memory of him until he come'. As he was for the first few decades of our era, he is no longer. We remember him until he comes, until the story that then received half an ending will close with his final return in glory. In one sense, he really is not here any longer. We might put that in another way: his earthly ministry is complete so that his heavenly one may be entered. As Paul says, he must reign until he has put all his enemies, and especially death, under his feet. That is the point of 'he sat': it is a change of *realm*, the place from which he rules.

We must not understand this crudely: neither does he go literally into outer space, as Luke's picture may suggest, nor does he literally sit on a throne beside an old man with a beard. By heaven is not meant a different place but a different *kind of* place altogether. For Scripture, 'heaven' is not 'up there' – though we cannot avoid the imagery of above and below – but the realm from which God rules his world. It is not a space separate from ours, but a place which embraces ours. We can speak of it in 'below' terms as well as 'above': 'underneath are the everlasting arms', another way of showing how God in his providence embraces our time and space, governing it in his own omnipotent and sovereign way – and that means through Jesus. That is the point about 'he sat': he took his place beside the Father, so that there might be one of us there – at the right hand of God the Father. This means that one who is truly one of us, Jesus, the crucified, is the one through whom God orders his world. This is the point of the imagery of the right hand, as in the expression, 'my right hand man'. Jesus, crucified, ascended and risen is the Father's right hand, just as our right hands – in my case, left – are the means by which we get things done in the world. (There is another hand, too; that we shall meet at the festival of Pentecost.)

2

But, as the first half of our text affirms, it is not any man who takes his place there. 'But when this priest had offered for all time one sacrifice for sins'. It is here that the contrast with Aaron, so important for this writer, comes in. Aaron is the

Ascension and the Perfect Sacrifice

shadow; he had to purify himself annually, and the annual Day of Atonement served only to do half the job. It had to be repeated, because it did not go to the heart. The blood of bulls and goats cannot cleanse the conscience from dead works. This priest offered *for all time* one sacrifice for sins. So, he is like Aaron in being a priest, unlike him in never having to repeat the offering. But why is that? Because the gift he gave was himself. He is at once high priest and victim, as the hymn which I should perhaps have chosen puts it:

> Thee we praise, high priest and victim,
> of our hearts the shepherd king.[1]

But how does that help?

3

We have to go back to the human condition to which Leviticus addresses itself. Human beings are called to be holy – that is, to be perfect before God – but we fail, polluting and diminishing ourselves by our sin. Thus our situation is, to use the fashionable word, dire. And our author says, only one can do anything about that, one who is both himself perfect and can carry over, transmit, his perfection to others. Such is Jesus, 'who, through the eternal Spirit offered himself unblemished [perfect] to God' (Heb. 9.14). But how does that help? One who has been through it all knows what it is like and can do precisely what is needed for those who struggle with the imperfection of our condition. Those words, 'through the eternal Spirit', are the clue to what we seek. The eternal Son of God, the one through whom God the Father made and upholds the world, empties himself to our estate, lives our life and dies our death. He is tempted and remains firm. He is opposed, betrayed, bullied, whipped and, at the last, as he goes, with eyes open, into the death that is prepared for sinners – though he had done no

---

1 *Rejoice and Sing*, 460. William Robinson (1888–1963), used by permission of the United Reformed Church.

wrong – he again resisted the temptation of the Devil to run away. Here is a man absolutely true to his calling, absolutely himself – 'Thou whose deeds and dreams were one'[2] – because he remains true to what he is, the Father's only and beloved Son, and to what he is called to be and do. And how? Hebrews tells us: through the eternal Spirit, the one who strengthened him when tempted and tortured, who led him through all that failure and pain and, finally, raised him from the dead, the firstborn of many brothers and sisters.

That is perfection, won through struggle against the powers of darkness, self-giving to the uttermost. And he can truly cleanse our hearts from dead works, because he goes on to pour out that Spirit by whom he was strengthened, led and raised. Only perfection can come into the presence of God, and, through him, we are given a promise that he is not the only one, but the firstborn. Notice the double emphasis of the final verse of the passage we heard from the great letter: 'by one sacrifice he has made perfect for ever those who are being made holy'. He has made perfect those who are being made perfect. By his death we are cleansed, our consciences set free; by his ascension we are promised that what he began in us, he will complete – and so we remember him, until he come – comes to complete his work, to offer us truly perfect before the throne of his Holy Father.

III

Last week in her sermon about the church as a building or temple, Lynn[3] made the absolutely correct point that we are all priests, all called to make our offering of praise and worship to God. The church is a kind of temple, made up of the living stones of God's people. The letter to the Hebrews puts the other side of that same point. We are priests because he was, we are the temple because he is, the one who perfects and completes all that God began with Aaron. In that confidence and hope, come to the table of our Lord.

---

2 *Rejoice and Sing*, 493.
3 Lynn Fowkes, the then minister of Brentwood URC.

24

The Remission of Sin

God made him who had no sin to be sin for us, so that in him we might become the righteousness of God.

(2 Cor. 5.21)

3 MARCH 2002

Readings: Hos. 6.1–7; 2 Cor. 5.13–21; Mt. 18.23–34

I

Perhaps the most important scene in Evelyn Waugh's *Brideshead Revisited* takes place by the fountain in the garden of the great country house – Castle Howard, almost certainly, in inspiration – which gives the novel its name. Julia Marchmain, a lapsed Catholic, is having an affair with the novel's narrator, but her Catholic past will not leave her alone. She becomes hysterical:

> 'Living in sin; not just doing wrong . . . doing wrong knowing it is wrong . . . *Living in sin*, with sin, always the same, like an idiot child carefully nursed, guarded from the world. "Poor Julia", they say, "she can't go out. She's got to take care of her sin. A pity It ever lived", they say, "but it's so strong . . . Julia's so good to her little, mad sin".'[1]

As an unbelieving non-Catholic, the narrator cannot begin to understand what is going on. Indeed, part of the book's theme

---

1 Evelyn Waugh, *Brideshead Revisited* (Harmondsworth: Penguin, 1962), p. 273.

is of Catholics who stand for a faith which nobody else understands, a beleaguered minority in a wicked and uncomprehending world, holding the fort against everybody else.

There are two things to be said about this. On the one hand is that the part of the book's theology which I found rather repellent is its rather rigid and mechanical view of sin, with the suggestion in its deathbed scene that the making of a small gesture before a priest at the point of death somehow qualifies the dying for heaven. And yet, on the other, it made me feel that we have now joined the Roman Catholics as those who do not belong in the modern world, with its increasingly pagan values. All Christians live now in a world where we are rendered a strange minority with apparently outmoded and unintelligible beliefs.

And, as with *Brideshead Revisited*, at the centre is the doctrine of sin. No Christian belief is stranger to the modern mind than the doctrine of sin. If used at all outside the church, it is used in a jokey way, of sexual relations, betraying an unease with the way they are conducted, but little more. If people offend against the law, statutory, religious or moral, they are unlikely to be classified as sinners. They are either victims of someone else, or sick and in need of therapy. There is, of course, some truth in all that: all sinners are victims, and all wrong-doing is also a kind of sickness. But to leave it there is to leave out a whole dimension of things. Anything that relieves people of their responsibility for what they are and do also relieves them of their humanity, for to be human is to be, among other things, responsible: responsible for what we are in our relations with our maker and what we do to one another. And in those responsibilities we all fall short, fail indeed. That is not to say that some are not greater sinners than others, but it does mean that all, without exception, are sinners, and all are accountable for their sin before the judgement seat of God.

But what is sin? Not, in the first place, particular sins like that of Julia Marchmain and Charles Ryder. Sin is, first of all, the way we stand before God – or fail to do so. Sin is throwing God's good gifts in his face, like Adam in the garden, who thought he knew better, and Israel in Hosea's account, loved as God's own people yet corrupting those gifts with infidelity and greed. Sin is, above all, what put Jesus on the cross. In the Gospel accounts, which we follow at this time of year as we prepare for Easter, we see what it means. He heals the sick; and he is accused of breaking the law. He welcomes the poor sinner and the rich tax collector, and he is accused of dirtying himself with the polluted. He tells the truth and is accused of devilry. He is the love of God in action, and he is put on the cross. Everything in the wrong place.

If we are to understand what is going on, we must remember that we are among the religious who did things like that and might well do them again. Karl Barth says that the essence of sin is to want to be our own God, to pronounce ourselves good and right and our neighbour wrong. And we do, when we carp and criticize and run down and gossip in order to make us feel better than our neighbour. Sin is what is unmasked when we sit at the foot of the cross and realize that we can plead nothing in our defence, certainly not that we have been victims of bad parents or an unjust social order, or whatever.

> When I survey the wondrous cross, on which the prince
>   of glory died,
> My richest gain I count but loss, and pour contempt on
>   all my pride.[2]

Sin is the human attempt to displace God from the centre of our lives and the consequent mess that results, ranging from unkind thoughts and words to the unhappiness, social disorder, oppression and war that they ultimately spawn.

---

2 *Rejoice and Sing*, 217.

II

We need to know all this and to realize that it means not other people but ourselves. And yet it is only the first thing that has to be said, not the second and not the last. The creed's only reference to sin is to confess the *remission* of sins: 'We confess one baptism for the remission of sin'. Sin is only known and acknowledged through its remission. And so we come to a text, 'God made him who had no sin to be sin for us, so that in him we might become the righteousness of God'. There are three clauses in this text, each of which would make a sermon in itself, but which I shall try to link together as clearly as possible. '[H]im who had no sin.' What does it mean that Jesus had no sin? It means, first of all, not that he committed no wrong acts but that his relation to God his Father was right, not wrong as ours is. That whereas we try to go our own way, to play God for ourselves and towards our neighbour, he was content – though by no means without a struggle – to do his Father's will, and nothing else. When tempted, he resisted; when wishing to run away from the task laid upon him, his final word was, 'Not my will but yours'. 'He knew no sin', because he lived all his life through the Spirit in obedience to his Father; he was thus innocent of all those things which lead to the hatred and the envy, the lust, theft, violence, greed and sloth which so disfigure our world.

Yet, the spotless lamb of God was 'made to be sin'. That is one of the most astonishing and offensive texts in the whole of Scripture, which has many of them. God made him to be sin, sent him to the fate – to the *death* – which is the inevitable outcome of sin. Notice it does not say that God punished him. Paul's word elsewhere is that he gave him up, made a sacrifice of him, as we might give up something precious for the sake of someone we love. God so loved the world, even the world which threw back his gifts in his face, that he gave up his only and beloved Son to death on the cross. He made him to be sin, allowed him to be treated among the sinners; he was, to use

The Remission of Sin

the Isaiah expression, numbered with the transgressors, although in no way did he belong there. Such love, of both the Father who gives up his Son and the Son who gives his life, is beyond our capacity to comprehend, although we can begin to, because we have such a wealth of poetry, art and song which seeks in so many ways to bring it home to us.

> Oh the sweet wonders of that cross
> where Christ my saviour loved and died.[3]

It is love which is the key to it, not the impoverished and selfish concept expressed in so much modern use of the word, but the love that gives all for the other. And it *was* all: 'he made him to be sin', gave him to take the place of those who had put themselves – or tried to put themselves – outside the love and care of God. He comes to where we are, so that we might be where he is.

And that takes us to the third clause we have to examine: 'so that we might become the righteousness of God'. Notice the contrast between his being made to be sin and our righteousness, our being right with God. He goes into the wrong place, so that we might be in the right one. He goes where God is not, the dreadful place of dereliction and death to which we condemn ourselves, so that we might be restored to our proper destiny as children of the one Father. There is an exchange, what an early writer called the 'sweetest exchange':

> In whom could we, lawless and impious as we were, be made righteous except in the Son of God alone? O sweetest exchange! O unfathomable work of God! . . . The sinfulness of many is hidden in the Righteous One, while the righteousness of the One justifies the many that are sinners.[4]

---

3 *Rejoice and Sing*, 219.
4 The so-called 'Letter to Diognetus'.

The word Paul uses for all this is reconciliation, another word, like love, which has suffered glib overuse. But it makes the same point: we change one place for another, we are taken out of the realm of death and hell to be God's beloved children, and, simply, because Jesus went to the cross for us. 'Amazing love, how can it be.'

III

And what does it mean for us? There is in literature one great image that helps us to see what this involves. John Bunyan's pilgrim approaches the cross of Christ, and, as he reaches it, a great burden which he is carrying on his back falls off and rolls away down the hill. Or there is Augustine's famous experience of conversion. Augustine was one of those tortured souls who found peace only in the Gospel. A rake as a young man – like so many brought up in the faith and rebelling against it – he tried several paths, but never faced up to the change required of him. And then he heard some children playing next door a game called 'take and read'. So he opened the Scriptures, and there read, 'not in orgies and drunkenness . . . Rather clothe yourselves with the Lord Jesus Christ, and do not think about how to gratify the desires of the sinful nature' (Romans 13.13–14). And he was changed, in the twinkling of an eye, freed to be a great servant of his Lord.

These images are important, because they see the remission of sins as the removal of a great burden. As Barth has said in the same context, it is a great burden to have to play God to ourselves and others. Remission of sins frees us to be simply human, to be those beings who let the love of God constrain us, to use Paul's way of putting it. But to see this primarily in terms of experiences of liberation or conversion can be misleading, for two reasons. The first is that we are all equally set free from our sins, but do not all experience our liberation in a sudden way. And the second is even more important: the remission of sins is not primarily an experience but being

The Remission of Sin

transferred to a new realm, to a new authority, a new sovereignty. That is the point of the reconciliation, the exchange. We are in a new place, and that is what matters. What counts is not what you feel – though it is good to feel set free from a burden – but where you are.

God rules the world through his Son Jesus Christ who died and rose, and the Spirit who holds us in his presence. By the power of that same Spirit, Jesus Christ meets us here, in his Word and through his sacraments. They are the two means whereby he becomes real for us. To hear his Word of grace and forgiveness week by week, and to have it set forth in bread and wine – what Augustine called visible words – is to continue to share in the remission of sins received in baptism. We continue to sin, and we shall until the day of our death, when we shall finally be set free to be fully the Lord's. But in the meantime, our sins do not need to control us, to decide who we are: in Christ we truly are the righteousness of God. So, eat and drink and be glad.

25

Judgement

There is indeed no single gift you lack, while you wait expectantly for our Lord Jesus Christ to reveal himself.

(1 Cor. 1.7)

ADVENT SUNDAY, 2 DECEMBER 2001

Readings: Isa. 64.1–9; 1 Cor. 1.1–9; Mk 13.24–7

I

We are, today, often urged not to be 'judgemental', by which I suppose is meant we should not be censorious about others' ways of living. Of course, even those who urge such are themselves judgemental about some people: those who hasten to approve every form of sexual excess, except perhaps child abuse, will almost certainly condemn racial discrimination. But behind all this, for all its hypocrisy (what someone once characterized as the moral spinelessness of the age masquerading as compassion) there is a theological truth: that only the God who knows the secrets of all hearts has the right to judge, to exercise the final judgement about right and wrong. We have to remember that there is a fine line between serious thought about right and wrong and the kind of censoriousness, which we all enjoy indulging in from time to time, that enables us to feel superior to those we may think of as lesser or less worthy mortals. It was after all Jesus who said that only those who are without sin have the right to cast the first stone.

The fact, however, is that we judge and are judged all the time, because we are so bound up with the lives of others that what they do affects us, and so we cannot but assess them. It is, however, without doubt, more healthy for us to be judged than to judge, to be measured against what we ought to be, simply because in the end we do not have a right to think others morally inferior to ourselves, and we need to see ourselves as others see us. Fortunately, life does judge us. It is full of what can be called provisional or penultimate judgements, matters in which we are tested, perhaps ways also through which the very shape of our lives is given. An examination is a case in point, but there are many things which are not formal examinations, but work like them, serve as examinations – of our courage, our tenacity, our love – and so enable us to make honest judgements about ourselves. Last Tuesday in studying Genesis's account of the call of Abraham, we noted that his faith was tested, twice at least. In that light, we could say that the whole of life is a kind of judgement, a testing by God of what mettle we are made.

'He shall come again in glory to judge both the living and the dead.' It is the claim of the creed that all these provisional judgements, these day-to-day tests of our mettle, will be rounded off in a final judgement. We shall be brought before the throne of our Father, and Jesus, the one who came at the first Christmas, will sift our works, to see which are worthy of the calling that we have each been given. Only then will our stories, and indeed that of the world, be complete. Only then will the whole story be known, as all the little examinations come together in a final assessment.

II

There are two ways of looking at the passage from 1 Corinthians which is set for the First Sunday in Advent. It can either be serious and say what it means or consist of heavy irony. Paul is about to lambaste – to be very judgemental indeed about – the life of the church at Corinth, as was his apostolic right and duty. The members – or some of them – were arrogant, quar-

Judgement

relsome and, indeed, thought that they had arrived to such a pitch of spiritual perfection that matters of right and wrong were indifferent to them. Is he then being sarcastic when he says in the opening greetings that 'I thank him [God . . . that] You possess all knowledge and you can give full expression to it'? At least one commentator thinks so, but that is probably not the case. There is undoubtedly an ironic undertone: Paul is going to tell them that they have got it all wrong. Yet he stresses that they have truly been endowed with the gifts of God – not something to boast about, but to accept as a gift.

Therefore, we should take it that in our text he is quite serious, as we can be sure that we are in the same position. These words are spoken to us. 'There is indeed no single spiritual gift you lack, while you wait expectantly for our Lord Jesus Christ to reveal himself.' The word sometimes translated 'spiritual gift' is the Greek 'charisma' – a gift of God, dependent on his giving for its proper use and yet a real gift nonetheless. However much Paul's churches fail, however much he has to tear a strip off their pretensions, he never denies that they are real churches with real gifts from God – gifts sufficient for all their needs.

However, one expression in this short passage introduces us to our Advent theme. 'There is indeed no single spiritual gift you lack, while you wait expectantly for our Lord Jesus Christ to reveal himself'. As you wait expectantly: here, as at many times of the church's history, there is eager expectation of something that is going to happen, apparently imminently. Notice the word that is used, 'as you wait . . . for our Lord Jesus Christ to be revealed'. 'To be revealed'? There is a similar expression in 1 Peter, making the same point in a similar situation, 'that your faith . . . may be proved genuine . . . when Jesus Christ is revealed', and the same expression recurs six verses later (1 Pet. 1.7, 13). But is Jesus not revealed already? In the manger, the teaching, the healing, the cross and the resurrection? Of course, but there only in hiddenness. It is quite possible to see in him a deluded fanatic, as many did, or a nuisance to the political peace of Israel or, in our age, as a figure lost in the mists of history, of no relevance to today. He is revealed indeed to the eyes of faith, as we shall see as once more we follow the wonderful story of Christmas during the next few weeks. But there is a different and absolutely inescapable revelation to come:

> Every eye shall now behold him
> robed in awesome majesty;
> those who set at naught and sold him,
> crucified him on the tree.

What was once hidden in the manger and the cross will be made known in all the world. We do not know how, or when this will happen. But we know that he who raised the crucified Jesus from the dead will see to it that his work is completed, both in each one of us and in his world.

There is one other important thing to notice in this text. The return of Christ in glory is not to be feared but to be welcomed. We shall see why later, but it is universal in the New Testament. It is something to be welcomed when this wicked world, torn with war and hatred and hunger and ignorance will finally be renewed through Christ, and the new heaven and earth, begun at the first Christmas, will be made perfect. The prayer at the end of the book of Revelation, that book written in and for a war- and persecution-torn world, is, 'Come, Lord Jesus'. Come and end our stories, cleanse and purify us of the sin that still clings so closely, so that we may be fit to enter the Father's kingdom. At Advent, we prepare ourselves for this, what we call the second coming, so that we may be made ready to celebrate the first coming at Christmas.

III

I spoke earlier about the many provisional examinations that we go through as our faith is tested and confirmed through our living out of the gospel. What we do here is chief among them. By sitting around the table of the Lord, we prepare for the final assessment that will be the outcome of the revealing of our Lord Jesus Christ in glory. Paul makes that clear later in the same letter. The situation is that the church's supper has been a source of conflict and division rather than of love and fellowship. And he tells the church: what they do in their life together is the acid test of their faith. The reason is that to eat the bread and drink the wine at the Lord's Supper in memory of the Lord is to undergo a kind of judgement. Those who undergo it unready for it – and he is referring to their disgraceful and drunken behaviour at the meal – endanger their very selves. It is a very serious matter. His words are difficult and obscure, but something like that underlies them, 'But if we judged (*diekrinomen*) ourselves, we would not come under judgement (*ekrinometha*). When we are judged (*krinomenoi*) by the Lord, we are being disciplined (*paideuometha*), so that we will not be condemned (*katakrithômen*) with the world' (1 Cor. 11.31–32).

The cup which we drink represents God's judgement. As he goes to the cross, Jesus accepts that he must drink the cup, the cup of God's wrath incurred by sinful man. By drinking it after him, we accept that our condition was bad enough for the Son of God to have to come to the world, to bear human flesh and to undergo death under divine judgement, though he had done no wrong. By eating and drinking here, we accept the condemnation that he bore, so that by living in and through him, we may be freed from it. We accept judgement – provisional, penultimate, judgement – so that we may be spared the ultimate rejection that is exclusion from the kingdom of the blessed; we are being disciplined (*paideuometha*), so that we will not be condemned (*katakrithômen*) with the world. We must not mistake what goes on here. It is clearly dangerous, for it is to undergo divine judgement – the judgement that we need if we are to be cleansed, but which will destroy us if it is not truly in Christ, in the reconciled community of his people.

But we do it gladly, knowing that our Lord has borne the judgement for us, already, in advance. Why then are we expected to look forward expectantly for the revealing of the Lord, like a child waiting for Christmas morning? It is clear that we shall undergo judgement, along with all the world. 'He shall return again in glory to judge both the living and the dead.' Is that not a threat? The right answer is that to be found in the 'He' who will return. Who is it? Not an angry deity but the one who died for us. Calvin puts it wonderfully, 'he appears before the Father's face as our constant advocate and intercessor . . . He fills with grace and kindness the throne that for miserable sinners would otherwise have been filled with dread'. Our judge will be the one who died for us, the vehicle of God's mercy.

He who testifies to these things says, 'Yes, I am coming soon'. 'Amen. Come, Lord Jesus' (Rev. 22.20).

Index of Biblical References

Genesis		
1		63, 122
1.1–13		3
3.17–24		87
29.10–28		133

Exodus		
6.2–13		81

Leviticus		
9.1–8		43
16.11–24		145

Deuteronomy		
7.7		18

2 Samuel		
7.1–11		37
7.16		37

1 Kings		
8.27		6
19.9b–11		49

2 Kings		
6.17		7
6.8–17		11

Psalms		
18		11
33.6		129
46.1–7		115
90.1–12		115
95		89
115.17		102
118		139

Isaiah		
40.1–11		109
45.1–8		61
47.12		56
49.1–7		67
55		123
60.1–6		55
64.1–9		159

Jeremiah		
31		18
31.15		68

Ezekiel		
36.22–8		127
37		26
47.1–12		121

Daniel		
12.1–10		101

Hosea		
6.1–7		151

Amos		
7.14		96

Micah		
5.1–5		75

Habakkuk		
1.12–2.3		95

Malachi		
3.1–5		31

Matthew		
1.20		39
2.1–12		55
2.13–23		67
13.24–30		49
13.37–43		49
18.23–34		151

Mark		
1.4–13		87
9.14–29		11
11.1–11		31
12		32
13.24–7		159
14.17–25		17

Luke		
1.26–38		37
7.29–35		43
8.40–2		3
8.49–56		3

13.1–9	61	11.25–36	75	**Hebrews**	
20.27–38	101	12.1–16	43	4.15	90
21.25–36	109	13.8–14	109, 156	9.11–15	17
24.27	70	16.7	34	9.14	41, 149
24.36–48	23			9.24–8	17
24.45–53	145	**1 Corinthians**		10.5–10	37
		1.1–9	159	10.11–12	145
John		7.30–31	113	11.1–10	11
1.13	40	9.1–14	31		
3.1–7	23	11.31–2	163	**1 Peter**	
4.24	130	13.1–13	133	1.7	161
7.30	85	15	70	1.13	161
7.37–44	121				
11.45–53	81	**2 Corinthians**		**Revelation**	
14.15–26	127	1.20	27	1.9–19	95, 127
19.10b–11a	83	5.13–21	151	4	97
20.1–18	139	8.9	45	5	97
				5.11–14	81
Acts		**Ephesians**		19.16	84
2	123	2.20	35	20.1–6	101
3.12–19	23	3.1–12	55, 67	20.11–15	101
10.34–43	139			21	100
		Philippians		21.1–14	49
Romans		1.15–26	115	22.1–7	121
4.16–25	3			22.20	164
5.12–17	87	**2 Thessalonians**			
8.11	124	2.1–12	61		